Owen Sheers is the author of two poetry collections, *The Blue Book* and *Skirrid Hill* (winner of the Somerset Maugham Award). His book about Zimbabwe, *The Dust Diaries*, won Wales Book of the Year 2005. His first novel, *Resistance*, has been translated into ten languages and was made into a film in 2011. Owen's plays include National Theatre Wales's *The Passion* and *The Two Worlds of Charlie F*, which won the 2012 Amnesty Freedom of Expression Award. His verse drama *Pink Mist* was recently short-listed for the BBC Drama Awards and won the 2013 Hay Medal for Poetry. Brought up in Abergavenny, Owen played scrum-half for Pontypool Colts, Blaina Youth, Gwent U17/18, New College Oxford and the University of East Anglia 1st XV.

Further praise for *Calon*:

'*Calon* is the product of Owen Sheers' year as writer-in-residence with the Welsh Rugby Union. Such appointments don't often yield much, but this is a marriage bred in heaven. Sheers brings to bear both the sensibility of a poet and the ubiquity of a scrum half (his position as an Abergavenny schoolboy) to encapsulate what it means to play for Wales or, from beyond the touchline, to root for Wales . . . Sheers captures the sense of the game's place in the culture and the landscape – in every Welsh fan's *calon* – with a lovely lyrical touch.' *Daily Telegraph*

'There's always been distinct poetry to the narrative of Welsh rugby: the bloodied aggression of legendary player JPR Williams buttressed by the songs of the supporters, more congregation than crowd. So it makes sense that a poet should explore the passion that makes Welsh internationals more than mere representatives of their country . . . There are plenty of sports books written by outsiders but it's a rare account that can marry such access with deeply thoughtful prose . . . It's beautiful but never cloying.' *Metro*

'Stirring imagery provides the poetic pulse of a book which considers Welsh rugby's cultural significance alongside the emergence of a national team that has thrilled and delighted fans in recent seasons . . . Admirers of Sheers's poetry and fiction, in which he's written about his native Wales, will relish his lyrical celebrations of the sport he loves . . . And Sheers's passion helps readers to invest emotionally in the team. Even though we already know the outcome, it's thrilling to read him describe Wales beating France to claim their third Grand Slam in eight years . . . After finishing this riveting hymn to the comradeship and claustrophobia of the Welsh team ethic, even English readers could catch themselves cheering on the Dragon.' Max Lui, *Independent on Sunday*

'[Sheers] has produced a remarkable insight into the existence of the modern sportsman . . . The story rattles along very nicely – even for readers without any loyalty to Wales or any interest in rugby. This is partly because it's a great story, and partly because Sheers takes the trouble to talk to people who normally fall below sports writers' radars . . . Sheers is a considerable talent, and this is a serious contribution to the literature of both Wales and its national sport. It will also help anyone who is keen to improve their knowledge of Welsh in ways not offered by road signs or announcements on Cardiff Central railway station.' Matthew Engel, *Financial Times*

'Everything he writes has a lyrical stamp of truth.' Jan Morris

'One of the finest writers at work today. He always finds the sublime in the everyday and the miracle in the mundane.' Michael Sheen

# CALON

## A Journey to the Heart of Welsh Rugby

OWEN SHEERS

FABER & FABER

First published in 2013
by Faber and Faber Limited
Bloomsbury House, 74–77 Great Russell Street
London WCIB 3DA
This paperback edition first published in 2014

Typeset by Ian Bahrami
Printed in the UK by CPI Group (UK) Ltd, Croydon CRO 4YY

A CIP record for this book
is available from the British Library

ISBN 978–0–571–29730–6

2 4 6 8 10 9 7 5 3 1

To Mr Jenkins, rugby coach
at KHS Comprehensive, Abergavenny,
and to all the other coaches
who keep the game alive.

'It's either the wedding game or the funeral game with us. Nothing in between.'

'Thumper' Phillips, Wales team manager

# TIME

## 17 March 2012

George North, a nineteen-year-old rugby player from Ynys Môn in North Wales, is packing his kitbag in a bedroom at the Vale Resort in Pontyclun, twelve miles west of Cardiff. He puts in two pairs of boots, a gumshield, recovery skins, a long- and a short-sleeved training top and a set of long studs. He checks the contents, then takes them out again, laying them on his bed. Pausing a moment, he puts them all back into the bag. Then he empties them onto the bed again.

George repeats this process five times before finally closing the bag, shouldering it and leaving the room. He's already written down his objectives for the match ahead on a piece of hotel notepaper. Having memorised this list of tactics and prompt words, he's ripped it up and thrown it in the bin. Before he did that, George phoned Andy McCann, a former Scottish karate international and stroke survivor who now works as a sports psychologist. Andy spoke with George about the match, but also about life outside rugby, about the flat George hoped to buy in Cardiff. With less than two hours to kick-off, just hearing Andy's voice is more important to George than anything he has to say about the game itself.

At six foot four and sixteen and a half stone, George, when running at full speed, summons one tonne of impact. He's an affable joker of a boy, effervescent with energy, quick to laugh or pull a face. Fluent in both Welsh and English, neither language seems capable of keeping up with the rapidity of his thoughts.

Since he was fifteen years old rugby has taken George away from his family. At first, living on his own was a struggle. He missed his parents and the island of Ynys Môn; washing his own clothes took time to master. But George wanted to play rugby at the highest level. So he moved south, into the heartland of Welsh rugby, where he trained and trained and played and played so that now, just four years later, here he is shouldering his kitbag and leaving his room at the Vale to board a coach with two red dragons painted down each of its sides.

Wales, like all nations, is an idea. A concoction of history, landscape, temperament and language. This afternoon George, and the twenty-one young men also boarding that dragon-painted coach, will become that idea. For eighty minutes, under the eyes of millions, they will become their country.

# Y FAN

'The new grass shall purge us in its flame.'
'Song at the Year's Turning', R. S. Thomas

It is five minutes to midnight in Cardiff on New Year's Eve 2011. Viewed from above, the streets of the Welsh capital are busy with light and movement. Taxis, cars, buses thread along Westgate Street and Cathedral Road. The crowds, impervious to a gauze of winter rain, thicken down St Mary's and Caroline Street, spilling into the smoking areas of clubs and bars. Mobile phones cast pale cauls across the downturned faces of drinkers sending texts. The organisers of firework displays check their watches and prepare their tapers. The city is charged with the year's turning, the birth and death of the annual calendar. A time for looking back, and for looking forward.

At the centre of all this activity, embedded in a crosshatch of headlights and a circuit board of street lights, one dimly lit oval is motionless. This is the Millennium Stadium, home to the Welsh rugby team. The yellow-green rectangle at its centre is the national pitch, semi-illuminated tonight by rows of growing lights suspended above the young grass.

From my position under the posts at the southern end of this pitch the intensity and number of these lights

3

resemble a huge theatrical rig dropped to within metres of the turf. The wheels of their structures look like the landing gear of aircraft, their rubber treads flecked with sand. The stands around me are dark. Only the exit signs hanging in each aisle remain lit, hundreds of white stick men running for their lives through the rows and rows of towering seats.

I am alone in an arena built for 75,000. Devoid of a crowd the stadium's atmosphere is like that of an empty theatre, quietly weighted with dormant purpose. In contrast, the streets beyond it are febrile with drink, music, bravado and lust. Even the outer corridors of the stadium have been permeated with the night's celebrations. As Gwyn, one of the stadium's security guards, led me towards the pitch earlier he explained that Level One of the building was being used as a triage centre – 'for the drinkers'. As we left his security lodge we'd passed through the chatter of personal radios angled at the shoulders of policemen and paramedics. Ambulance drivers in fluorescent jackets cradled mugs of tea beneath rows of framed and signed rugby shirts. A girl in a black mini-dress was slumped in a wheelchair, one of her high-heeled shoes missing, like a comatose Cinderella. A nurse pushing through a set of swing doors revealed a glimpse of the hospital beds beyond.

As I followed Gwyn down an echoing corridor, the noises of the triage centre faded behind us. We passed glass cabinets displaying boxing gloves, track shoes, rugby balls, boots, corner flags, before coming to a huge silver dragon on the wall, its clawed foot raised. Taking a short flight of stairs up past this dragon we came to the double doors of the players' tunnel. Pulling on one of these doors, Gwyn, like a New York porter welcoming a guest, gestured towards the massive interior–exterior that is the stadium's bowl, his hand open in invitation. 'The stadium, Mr Sheers,' he said, with more than a hint of mischief, 'is yours.'

With Gwyn closing the door behind me I walked down the shallow gradient of the tunnel, the pitch faintly lit at its end. With every step the stadium's stands grew around me, rising together to frame a rectangle of night sky, mirroring the rectangle of turf beneath. Emerging from the tunnel I was met not by the sea-like roar of a capacity crowd greeting a player making his entrance, but by silence. A huge, open crucible of silence. The empty stadium was all I could see, at once imposing and comforting; a 75,000-seat embrace. And not one inch of it tonight, whatever Gwyn said, was mine.

And nor is it anyone else's. Because if you are Welsh and a rugby fan, then you'll know the Millennium Stadium is, by its very nature, 'ours', and that it's from this plurality the building derives its significance. Without 'us' or 'ours', the stadium is a shell. As the late Ray Gravell, rugby player, druid, actor, once said: 'Remember, the people make the place.'

The Welsh for those last two words, 'the place', is '*y fan*', a translation that makes this stadium a rich meeting point for the two languages of Wales, coming together between these stands to depict, at one and the same time, the people and the place, the place and the people.

Standing under the posts at the southern end of the stadium I look out at the pitch as it glows eerily in the night. I know I'm meant to stay off the grass. But the temptation to walk, just once, the length of the national ground is overwhelming. I've only ever shared this space with thousands of other supporters. I feel a strange mix of privilege and trespass, as if I've stolen this moment and I'm committing a crime in being here. But as a lifelong supporter of the Welsh rugby team, as the man who still remembers the boy who first watched Wales play from the schoolboy enclosure of Cardiff Arms Park, the stadium's previous incarnation, the temptation is too much. So I walk.

As I pass under the first growing lights their heat pulses across the top of my head. At the twenty-two-metre line I see a spider's web strung between one of their tubular struts, its fine strands hung with rain. I walk on towards the last row of lights on the halfway line, then continue into a deepening darkness until, a hundred metres later, I'm standing under the posts at the other end of the stadium. Turning round, I look back down the pitch, bisected now by the dark trail of my own footsteps. Seeing them, I feel as if I haven't just walked across the national ground, but across the national *ground*; as if I've traversed Wales itself.

In reality I've just walked across some of the 7,412 removable pallets that make up this pitch, each packed with soil, sand and Lytag, a lightweight aggregate made from pulverised fuel ash. Each pallet is topped with 40 mm of turf seeded with a mix of meadow and rye grass from Scunthorpe, not Wales. But like all stadia the Millennium Stadium is a transformative space. The majority of its existence is spent waiting for certain dates when matches will be played within its stands. When those matches happen, things change, and when they are Welsh matches, they change even more. Individuals become a crowd, but also a nationality; the players in the dressing rooms become a team, but also a country; and the turf on the pitch becomes territory, but also *tir*, the Welsh for 'ground'.

Welsh players are reminded of this last transformation in a statement written above their changing stalls in the home dressing room. On one wall, in metre-high red writing over the heads of the props and the back rows, they're asked to 'RESPECT THE JERSEY'. On the other, above the heads of the centres and wingers, as they check their studs and their strappings, equally large letters spell out '*DAL DY DIR*' – 'Hold your ground'.

In Welsh, the double meaning of that last word is more potent than in English, denoting 'land' as much as 'ground'. But as I look back down the pitch I find myself wondering if another word, '*pridd*', meaning 'earth' or 'soil', isn't better suited to the transformation this turf

7

undergoes when played on by Wales. The etymology of '*tir*' is Latinate, relating to '*terra firma*', or the French '*terroir*'. '*Pridd*', however, predates Latin. It's a purely indigenous word and, as such, its greater depth, of both origin and meaning, is perhaps more evocative of the kind of cultural excavation experienced by a home crowd when they watch Wales play.

I am more than a little drunk. It is New Year's Eve and I've been celebrating the fact for the last five hours. I know, however, that my thoughts aren't fuelled by new-year alcohol alone, but also by years of association with the team who call this stadium home. This is the place where, over the last thirty years, I've felt myself most obviously Welsh. Where I've allowed myself to sink unashamedly into a nationalism I'd find unpalatable in any other area of my life. Where I've felt myself become more than myself, and where, in the opening minutes of a match, I've indulged in the kind of outrageous amnesia and hope of which perhaps only the devout sports fan is capable.

And, of course, I'm not alone. For almost as long as the game has existed, Wales has been synonymous with rugby. As early as 1891, just ten years after the formation of the Welsh Rugby Union, the *South Wales Daily News* identified rugby as 'the one great past time of the people'. Rugby is the foundation sport of Welsh culture. Each year the nation's psychological well-being is held ransom to the fortunes of the national squad. In return, the players and coaches of that squad are subjected to endless enquiry, expectation and obsessive support.

As I stand alone in the Millennium Stadium in the dying minutes of 2011, I know all of this to be true. And yet, as I look up at the struts of the posts tapering into the night above me, I also know it to be ridiculous. None of it, looked at coldly, makes any sense. Why should the Welsh, a predominately working-class nation, have chosen to identify themselves through the lens of rugby union, a predominately upper-class sport? What is it about the game that speaks so powerfully to the Welsh psyche? Why should a game of fifteen men trying to place an oval ball across their opponents' line, which in the broad view of the world doesn't matter at all, within Wales matter so much?

If you're a Welsh rugby fan, you'll *feel* the answers to these questions more than know them. You'll sense intuitively there's something in the game that makes it appear organically grown from the character of Wales. But it wasn't.

Other than perhaps the medieval inter-parish contests of *cnappan*, in which thousands on foot and horseback competed for a wooden ball boiled in tallow, the rules of modern rugby union have no indigenous roots in Wales. The sport as played today evolved from a variety of competitive ball games encouraged by masters of nineteenth-century English public schools, partly as a way of marshalling an increasing tide of riotous behaviour. Between 1768 and

9

1832 there were twenty-one public-school rebellions in England. A riot at Rugby school provoked a reading of the Riot Act and the attendance of soldiers with drawn swords. Another saw mass expulsions in its wake. Organised sport, especially of a rigorous nature, was considered a useful outlet for such violent energies.

It was a professor of Hebrew who brought rugby to Wales. The Rev. Rowland Williams was a fellow and tutor at King's College Cambridge when Albert Pell, an ex-Rugby pupil, introduced his school's variety of football to the university. Williams, in turn, introduced the game to St David's College, Lampeter, when he became Vice Principal there in 1850. Over the next twenty years this pattern was repeated across Wales, with returning teachers and headmasters introducing the game to educational establishments after exposure to 'Rugby's' football at universities across England and Scotland. Llandovery College, Christ College Brecon, Cowbridge Grammar, Monmouth School: these were some of the first rugby clubs in Wales. When pupils left these schools, they formed the foundations of town clubs such as Chepstow, Llandaff and Cardigan. A sport which had its genesis on the playing fields of English public schools was spreading through Wales along similar educational lines.

The touchpaper of popular enthusiasm, however, like the traditional beacons of the Welsh hills, would be lit on higher ground than these lowland clubs. It wouldn't be fuelled by the pupils and staff of schools, but by the working men of factories, mines and ports. In the last third of the nineteenth century the South Wales valleys experienced industrialisation on a massive scale. In 1840 four and a half million tonnes of coal were mined in the area. By 1913 almost fifty-seven million tonnes were produced. Migrant workers poured into the valleys from rural Wales and across the English border. Over these years only the United States attracted immigrants at a higher rate. This growing population, adjusting to the new rhythms and regulation of industrialised work, were hungry for a sport that matched the physicality and regimentation of their new lives. The new game of rugby football fitted the bill and quickly became an integral part of Welsh working-class culture. Support for the game came from their bosses too, with captains of industry realising, perhaps like those English headmasters before them, that rugby could be a useful method of control for a potentially fractious workforce.

The new communities of the valleys were created without a bedrock of generations. They had to design the architecture of their own identities. As towns such as Blaina, Pontypridd and Tredegar grew through the last decades of the nineteenth century, so did their communal institutions, each a projection of that town's personality. Brass bands, choral societies, darts clubs, miners' institutes, pigeon and greyhound racing all flourished, and, as the ultimate expression of communal loyalty, so too did rugby clubs. The same was true of the port towns fed by the valleys' industry: in Newport, Cardiff and Swansea rugby came to represent a powerful form of communal expression. As the industrial towns and populations grew ever closer to each other, the rugby field became the place where your efforts, hopes and allegiances could still be pledged to something more local, something that spoke of where you came from and who you were.

But it wasn't just local identities that found expression through rugby. The rising popularity of the sport also tracked a parallel movement of increasing national confidence. With her new prosperity and dynamism, Wales in the late nineteenth century was emerging, after years of being overshadowed by her imperial neighbour, as a distinct modern entity. In 1872 the first University College of Wales was founded in Aberystwyth, with Cardiff and Bangor following suit. Campaigns for a national library and museum began in the 1870s. A new regiment, the South Wales Borderers, fought in the Zulu wars of 1879. The National Eisteddfod Society was founded in 1880, and in February 1881 the first Welsh rugby team lined up against England at Blackheath. Fielding something of a scratch side, with two players recruited from the crowd, Wales were soundly beaten by eight goals and six tries to nil. The following month, at the Castle Hotel in Neath, the Welsh Rugby Union was formed.

A hundred and thirty years later, the stadium in which I'm standing tonight is testament to that union's success.

With its position in the centre of the city, where a cathedral or a parliament might usually stand, it's an eloquent embodiment of the place rugby occupies in Welsh culture. But why does rugby occupy that place? And why do the origins of the game continue to invest the sport with such meaning in Wales?

The most persistent resonance is a question of class. When a dispute over professionalism saw the northern English clubs break away from the Rugby Football Union in 1895, only Wales was left with a working-class rugby-union ethos. In northern England the new professional rugby league became dominant, while in southern England, Scotland and Ireland the union game played second fiddle to the populist sports of soccer and Gaelic football. Rugby union remained the preserve of public schools, universities and white-collar society. In Wales, however, the lifeblood of rugby continued to flow from the industrialised valleys and port towns, the ball passing through hands that spent the rest of their time cutting and hauling coal, rolling steel or loading ships.

The other home nations weren't always comfortable with this class distinction. At the turn of the century there were even complaints that Wales had an unfair class advantage. As working men, it was argued, the Welsh were able to get into better condition than their amateur gentlemen opponents. At the 1903 AGM of the Irish RFU it was noted that:

Over £50 had been paid for a dinner to the Scotsmen and only £30 for a dinner to the Welshmen. The reason for this was that champagne was given to the Scotsmen and beer only (but plenty of it) to the Welshmen. Whisky and porter were always good enough for Welshmen, for such were the drinks they were used to. The Scotsmen, however, were gentlemen, and appreciated a dinner when it was given to them. Not so the Welshmen.

The early association of rugby with a renewed sense of national identity also continues to contribute to its contemporary resonance in Wales. George Borrow, the nineteenth-century travel writer, wrote in his book *Wild Wales* that the Welsh character was partly shaped by the fact that 'the Welsh have never forgotten they were conquered by the English, but the English have already forgotten'. With rugby's territorial contest of possession and confrontation, Wales was gifted a communal way to continue that never forgetting. On a rugby field the knowledge that the Welsh and their language are stubborn survivors of a pre-Anglo-Saxon Britain is a rich seam of national consciousness which even in the twenty-first century is still evoked and defended every time Wales take the field.

Then there is the question of scale. Wales has always been a small nation. With a population of just three million, the country can draw upon roughly the same number of players as Yorkshire. Its diminutive size means matches against opponents such as England, Ireland and France have always been laced with the potency of a David versus Goliath narrative, however much the bookies or the fans might favour Wales.

To what extent class, history and size are at the forefront of a twenty-first-century Welsh supporter's mind as they watch a Wales match today is debatable. But what *is* certain is that this cultural heritage is still inherited and therefore, at the very least, still sensed. Similarly, a twenty-first-century Welsh player can't escape the traditions they pull on with their jersey. Their minds might be occupied with video analysis, nutrition, team policy, tactics and preparation, but however diffuse the hinterland of Welsh rugby's earliest days might be, it's still a part of what fuels the modern player. Even those who play with individuals more than a nation in mind, those who take the field for the grandfathers, mothers, coaches who've helped them on their way, those individuals will all, in some way, have embodied the national ethos of the game. All of which goes to explain why it's never just a country that runs out onto this pitch at the Millennium Stadium, but a culture, a way of being. Every match played by the national side is an act of national memory.

Over the last few years, as Welsh players have pulled on their jerseys in the dressing rooms they'll have glimpsed a word printed inside their collars. The jersey itself will have been made by an American company, Under Armour, constructed from some of the most high-tech materials of the twenty-first century. The military-grade fabric will feature ArmourGrid technology and body-mapped compression insets. The word inside each collar, though, will be thousands of years old and a reminder of the latticework of history and culture that's still woven into what it means to play rugby for Wales.

Between 2008 and 2010 the word players saw inside the collar of their home shirt was '*Calon*', meaning 'heart'. In their away strip it was '*Hiraeth*', meaning 'a longing for something lost'.

From 2010 to 2011 they were reminded again, inside their home shirts, to '*Dal dy Dir*' – 'hold your ground' – while in the away collar they wore '*Balchder*' – 'pride'.

Since 2011 the word players will have seen when pulling on their black away shirts is '*Cymeriad*' – 'character'. Inside their red home shirts it is '*Braint*', meaning 'privilege'.


Midnight.

A wave of cheers washes into the stadium from the streets of Cardiff beyond. 2012 has arrived. The first fireworks shoot into the night sky and explode in reds, greens and gold. In the empty bowl of the stadium, resonating between the stands, they sound like cannon fire. A rapid fusillade of smaller rockets crack and whistle from elsewhere in the city, disturbing a seagull from its perch in the stadium's roof. As it flies over me the growing lights on the pitch briefly illuminate it from underneath, casting its feathers as pristine as a player coming off the bench. More fireworks erupt in other areas of the city. The year has turned.

For the current Welsh squad, this new year poses a question first formed under the floodlights of another pitch on the other side of the world in what is now, just, last year. Wales were playing France at Eden Park in Auckland in the semi-finals of the Rugby World Cup. Commentators were calling it the biggest game in the history of Welsh rugby. Not just because the squad were eighty minutes from a final against the hosts, New Zealand, but because never before had a World Cup semi-final pointed so strongly towards a Welsh victory. France had been off form. Their tournament had been erratic and distracted. Virtually estranged from their coach, the team had yet to discover the rhythm or the flair that had seen them do so well in previous World Cups.

Wales, by contrast, despite fielding eight players under the age of twenty-three, had been the team of the tournament. For the first time in their history the national coach, Warren Gatland, had had the squad for two clear months of preparation. They'd twice travelled to gruelling training camps at Spała in Poland, where, with the aid of regular three-minute sessions in the −150°C cryotherapy chambers, they'd trained harder and more often than any other Welsh squad had ever trained before.

Rugby coaches often talk about 'strength in depth': developing enough quality players to cover injuries to the first-choice team. In Poland, however, Wales were developing a different kind of strength and depth. Under the eye of Adam Beard, the team's head of physical performance, the players' bodies were being strengthened to the point where, as centre Jamie Roberts put it, 'you're thinking about your next move, not your next breath'. But the Spała experience was also about developing depth – of resolve and attachment.

The modern top-flight rugby player is often a hard man who leads a soft life. At a young age he'll have life experiences most of us will never know, and yet his experience of life will be relatively narrow. While their peers are going through an expansion of independence, the young rugby professional experiences a contraction. Much of their day-to-day lives is organised by someone else. Travel and schedules are set, day sheets appear under hotel doors, food and drink is monitored. They are given the best treatments and good salaries, but they also no longer work side by side for long hours in mines, fields or factories.

Warren Gatland and his team knew that Wales had often lost key games in the closing minutes. When the time had come to dig deep, that depth wasn't there. At Spała, where Adam Beard says he pushed the squad '150% harder than ever before', the players hurt, and they hurt together. As one group waited for another to finish a session, there was silence in the room, such was the anxiety about what lay ahead of them. In the relatively simple surroundings of the camp, with no TV or computer games, they spent time together too. They talked, played cards and competed in quizzes. In previous squads there had always been some fighting between the players. But in Spała there was none. On their one day off, many chose to visit the nearby concentration camp at Auschwitz.

The Olympic Sports Centre in Spała was founded in 1950. Despite recent developments it still resembles a training camp for Soviet cosmonauts. Situated a hundred kilometres south-west of Warsaw, its buildings are located within hectares of oak forests through which herds of European bison once roamed. The village of just four hundred inhabitants is dominated by the centre's presence. The ceiling of the nearby Olympic Pizzeria is papered with the front pages of a newspaper called *Sport*, while its menu offers a range of dishes all named after Olympic cities.

The centre's three simple hotels – Champion, Junior and Olimpijczyk – sit squarely and heavily between its facilities of indoor and outdoor running tracks, gyms, a cavernous sports hall, swimming pool, treatment rooms and – Wales's chief reason for being there – cryotherapy chambers. In their preparation for the World Cup the Welsh players stripped off twice a day to enter the icy vapour of these liquid-nitrogen-cooled freezers. Wearing just a pair of shorts, long woollen socks, gloves, face mask, headband and wooden clogs, their blood pressures were taken by a nurse before they stepped, in groups of six, into the preliminary cooling chamber. A computer beside the chamber recorded its temperature as −50°C. The players crossed their arms, covering their nipples with their gloved hands as a member of staff dressed for an Arctic expedition opened the door to the secondary chamber. Outside on the computer screen the temperature in this second chamber can read anywhere from −120°C to −150°C.

Inside, it is a white-out. On stepping into this second chamber the players immediately lose sight of each other, their bodies lost in the freezing vapour. The sounds from beyond the chamber are muffled. Those inside have to keep talking to check in on each other, each man rocking from side to side or walking a tight pattern of steps. The cold is clean, dry and penetrating. The players' brains, suddenly alert through instinctive survival, cause their blood vessels to contract and send endorphins streaming through their systems and blood rushing to their cores. Their skin temperature drops to below 12°C and the seconds begin to lag as any residual moisture – in the backs of the legs, in the crook of an arm – stings sharply. With a minute to go some of the players' teeth are chattering. Others have broken into involuntary shivers. Eventually, the heavy metal door opens with a thick clunk and the players file into the preliminary chamber, then, after a few seconds' acclimatisation, out into the warmth, a flood of dry ice blowing out with them around their legs into the room.

After each of these cryotherapy sessions the squad took to the bikes and rowers in the gym across the corridor. With the stereo turned up they did twenty minutes of gentle exercise, pumping the blood through their veins to achieve the 'vascular flush' which would complete the treatment's rehabilitation of their damaged tissues. The fundamental science behind this method is the same as that which has seen sports teams use ice baths and other cold therapies for many years. The aim is to reduce inflammation, produce endorphins and dampen the nervous system. By shortening recovery periods the players can do harder training sessions, more frequently. An ice bath, however, causes stress to a player's skin. In reaction their blood, before flooding to the core, first rushes to the surface. The shock also produces stress hormones such as cortisol, which can counteract the benefits of the treatment. For the Welsh players, who can have as much as four inches of muscle packed about their limbs, there is also the question of penetration. An ice bath may only affect the first two inches of soft tissue, leaving deeper tissue still inflamed and damaged.

Whatever the science or the balance of the physical and psychological effects, the squad in Spała soon became convinced there was no way they could have trained as hard as they did without the cryotherapy. In some weights sessions they lifted as much as four tonnes each. Every day they undertook levels of fitness training that would usually have left them aching all over with 'the DOMS' (Delayed Onset Muscle Soreness). The cryo, however, had them waking each morning feeling refreshed and able to continue with Adam's punishing regime. Coaches often talk about muscle memory, but the use of cryotherapy at Spała was more about muscle amnesia: about wiping away the residue of physical exertion to leave the effect but not the ache, the gain but not the pain.

When not training inside at Spała, the squad worked on a pitch in front of Hotel Junior ringed by a running track and overlooked by a statue embedded in the corner of Hotel Champion. Sculpted in the Soviet style, a male figure places one hand on his chest, while the other holds aloft a flaming torch which he looks towards in aspiration. Next door to the training pitch, also under this statue's gaze, the Park Pokoleń Mistrzów Sportu commemorates Polish Olympic champions such as Jan Mulak, Irena Szewińska and Wanda Panfil.

On the pitch itself the Welsh squad often trained under the eye of a man who has had his own fair share of Olympic experience. Frans Bosch is one of the world's leading experts on biomechanics. Specialising in the high jump, he has coached many athletes to Olympic level, using his techniques of fine-tuning running efficiency to improve their performances dramatically. As the Welsh players ran through their moves on the pitch in Spała, Frans, with his shoulder-length hair and salt-and-pepper stubble, moved among them, watching with both the eye of an expert and that of an artist.

Before he became a specialist in physical training, Frans was, for twenty years, a well-known painter. Although he turned his back on his exhibitions and paintings before some of these Welsh players were born, he still draws as much upon his artistic experience as his scientific. 'It's about how you see movement,' he explains. 'An artist's eye is trained to renew the perception of what you see time and time again. If you can do that with looking at running, then human running is one of the most remark-able movement patterns there is. Renewing what you see helps to find the errors and how they are connected, and how best they can be corrected.'

Frans has no national allegiance to Wales and he thinks rugby is 'a pretty ridiculous sport'. Yet every time he trains with the Welsh squad he finds himself rooting for them beyond a professional interest. Compared to other 'more corporate' teams with whom he's worked, he can't help but warm to the 'family coherence' of the Wales set-up and to the national love of rugby as a sport. 'I went to watch a match in Cardiff', he says, 'and I realised I was seeing the country, not a sport. A cultural event, not a game.'

At the Rugby World Cup in New Zealand Wales's performance proved Warren and his team had been right to follow their instincts in Spała. After a narrow defeat by just one point to a vastly more experienced South African side, the young Welsh squad displayed a mature determination in convincingly beating Samoa, Fiji, Namibia and Ireland. Before the tournament most of the squad were unknowns on the international stage: Rhys Priestland, Dan Lydiate, George North, Leigh Halfpenny, Jonathan Davies. A few years earlier many had been playing schoolboy rugby, and yet now the rugby world was talking about them, and not just because of their wins, but because of the manner of those wins; because of their style of play and their demeanour on and off the pitch.

Ever since rugby union went professional in 1995, every Welsh team has had to negotiate a delicate balance between tradition and innovation. The shadow of the great teams of the 1970s still falls across a twenty-first-century squad. Many of those 1970s players are still present in the consciousness of the rugby public, as commentators, journalists, board members and coaches. The Welsh supporter demands a style of play, a philosophy, inherited from that Welsh rugby past: inventive and audacious, physical yet graceful. But at the same time there is now the pressure to compete at the leading edge of the sport, to 'pinch an inch' wherever possible in a game so much harder, faster and more brutal than the rugby of the 1970s, 1980s or 1990s. Cryotherapy, analysis, nutrition, sports science, GPS positioning, psychology:

the modern Welsh team, while aware of its heritage, has to be ever more forward looking.

In the Barn, the indoor training area at the Welsh Rugby Union's National Centre of Excellence in the Vale of Glamorgan, two massive banners hang side by side above the expanse of emerald AstroTurf:

YESTERDAY IS IN THE PAST

HOW DO YOU WANT TO BE REMEMBERED?

*Forget the past and live for the moment*, the first seems to say.

*Think of your legacy, the presence of what has been, forged in your now*, says the other.

As the Welsh squad do their drills and units in the Barn, they run between these two banners. Playing miss moves, set pieces, rucks and attacks they flow from one to the other as if the whole building is being rhythmically tipped from side to side. As a team and as individuals they shuttle between a statement and a question, between the past and the future.

At the 2011 World Cup Wales hit a balance between those two competing states. They arrived at the tournament as one of the most sophisticated sides of the twenty-first century. Their youngest players had graduated through the academies of professional clubs, travelling in a gilded channel of top-level rugby since the age of fifteen or sixteen. And yet something in the squad's personality, in the positivity of their play, still spoke strongly of the Welsh rugby past that fed their Welsh rugby present.

The character of the squad was embodied by their captain, Sam Warburton, who at twenty-two was the youngest-ever captain of a World Cup side. At six foot two and sixteen stone three pounds Sam is a relentless, scavenging open-side flanker. Against South Africa he personally made almost a quarter of Wales's ninety-nine tackles. Physically imposing, a man of few words with a craggy, Roman profile, Sam leads by example. A teetotaller with a highly developed sense of duty and fairness, he's the first onto the training pitch, the first to put on his recovery skins, to make his protein shake or to fill the ice bath. Under his captaincy 'no sapping' became the ethos of the team. If you're hurting, tell the physios, but not your teammates. If you're tired, tell the conditioning coaches, but not the other players. If the English squad at the tournament were displaying the qualities of Prince Hal in *Henry IV Part I* – going out drinking, being careless with their reputations – then Sam and his team were more like the young king of *Henry IV Part II*: determined, ruthless and choosing to harness their youth for the fight, not the revels.

When Sam and his twin brother Ben were born five weeks premature, the maternity nurse tried to explain the situation to Sam's parents. 'Let's put it this way,' she said.

'They're never going to be rugby players.' Seven years later, as his mother was putting him to bed, Sam remembers talking to her about what he might be when he was older. 'I want to be a footballer,' he told her from his pillow. 'Why?' she asked him. 'Well,' he replied. 'I'm never going to be a rugby player, am I?'

But Sam was fast, frequently winning the sports-day sprints, and his junior-school teacher, Frank Rees, was a rugby man. When Sam finally listened to Frank's encouragement and played for his school against Willowsbrook, he scored four of the team's tries. Willowsbrook's teacher coached for Cardiff schools and knew a good player when he saw one. Within weeks Sam was playing for Cardiff.

On his fifteenth birthday Sam's parents gave him a multigym, which he set up in their garage in Whitchurch. He knew he had to bulk up and get fit for rugby, so whenever he could he lifted weights in that garage or went running in the streets. As he ran, dreaming of playing for Wales, Sam listened to 'Refuse to Be Denied', a song by Anthrax, his father's favourite metal band.

Seven years later, on the night of 15 October in Auckland, as he sat in the changing rooms of Eden Park preparing to captain Wales in the biggest game of their history, Sam listened to that song again. With his head bowed and the headphones snug over his ears, the lyrics of his childhood, the lyrics that had accompanied him through countless weights sessions and through the night-time streets of Whitchurch, spoke to him once more:

Refuse to be denied,
Refuse to compromise.

When the Welsh squad first gathered at Spała, Warren and his assistant coach Rob Howley had spoken to the players about it being their destiny to meet New Zealand in the final of the World Cup. It was a private, in-camp conversation, informed by what the coaches knew about their young side's potential and the training ahead of them in Poland. As the World Cup progressed, however, that private conversation became increasingly, in the eyes of the rugby-watching world, a public expectation.

All sports fans have a love of narrative, for the stories that feed into key matches, big fights or prize-winning races. They are the stories that raise the stakes and heighten the enjoyment of sport's vagaries. For rugby fans in the autumn of 2011 that story had become the rise of a young Welsh side towards a tantalising final against the tournament's hosts, the New Zealand All Blacks. Wales's place in the final began to feel deserved, somehow *right*. Support spread far beyond national borders, with even former English players such as Will Greenwood tweeting in the minutes before the France match, 'I want to be Welsh!'

The destiny of which the Welsh coaches had spoken in Spała was now, in the hours before kick-off, being spoken of by the rest of the world.

*

The last of the fireworks have fallen. 2012 is only ten minutes old and already the excitement of its birth is ebbing. The streets beyond are subdued, and the stadium falls back into a strangely natural soundscape: the running of rainwater in the storm drains, a cave-like dripping in the stands, the occasional creak of an aisle sign like the groan of a branch in the wind.

Two and a half months ago, on the night of Wales's semi-final against France, this empty pitch in front of me was filled with Welsh rugby supporters. Thousands more sat up in the stands, their Welsh jerseys rashing the stadium red. In all, 65,000 fans came here to watch Wales that night, even though their team was playing on the other side of the world. But this was no ordinary match. This was a match to be shared. And so the fans came, to watch together under the stadium's closed roof as the game was screened at either end of the pitch. Undiluted by supporters of another team, never before had so many voices sung the Welsh national anthem in this stadium. Half a world away the Welsh team, lined up on the pitch at Eden Park, their arms about each other's shoulders, also sang. And in the Red Lion pub on Bleeker Street in New York, and in the Three Kings in London, and on Aviano air base in Italy and Camp Bastion in Afghanistan, and in homes and pubs and rugby clubs across the world, Welsh supporters sang. Because whatever the time of day, the story of this game was just too good to miss.

But it was also too good to be true.

The script of a rugby match is written not by prophecy or hope, but by the second. And a second was all it took for Wales's story to change that night; the 1,061st second, when Sam Warburton, refusing to be denied, threw the full force of his weight into a tackle on the French winger, Vincent Clerc.

When the Frenchman received the ball from a line-out, Sam had been waiting for him, crouched in anticipation. Wrapping his arms about his waist and pulling at the backs of Clerc's thighs, Sam straightened from his crouch to drive his right shoulder up and under the winger's ribcage. At just fourteen stone, two stone lighter than Sam, Clerc was lifted into the air, his feet swept up over his head. As he fell backwards towards the ground, head and shoulders first, Sam's grip loosened as if he already knew, even before Clerc had landed, what he'd done.

Immediately the Welsh and French forwards tightened around the point of collision, running in to shove and pull at each other's jerseys. Wales's Luke Charteris pulled Sam from the melee as the referee, Alain Rolland, blew on his whistle three times to break up the arguing players. Clerc lay on his back behind the scuffle, the French doctor and physio kneeling beside him.

Reaching into his pocket, Rolland pulled out a red card and showed it to Sam, pointing with his other hand off the pitch. He was sending Sam off for an illegal tip tackle. Sam walked to the touchline, his head bowed, and sat in one of the sub's chairs. Someone placed a tracksuit across his shoulders, someone else ruffled his hair. But Sam just looked out onto the pitch, his chest still heaving with the effort of the game, trying to take in what had happened. Wales, with just a 3–0 lead and sixty minutes of the semi-final still to play, were without their captain and down to fourteen men.

Across the world commentators and fans were complaining about the harshness of Alain Rolland's decision. Online a flurry of protests broke out on forums and websites covering the match. A yellow card, it was felt, would have been fair. The tackle had gone too far, but there'd been nothing malicious in Sam's intent. When Sam himself, however, was shown an image of the incident, he immediately accepted Rolland's call and said he saw no reason to appeal, accepting the citing board's judgement of a three-week ban.

In most rugby matches, on being presented with an advantage like Sam's sending off the opposing team would pile on the points. In international rugby, to lose a man like Sam is to lose strength in the scrum, dominance at the breakdown, cover in defence and support in attack. It is to unlock the door of victory for your opponent. Somehow, though, Wales held on and the match remained close. But their rhythm was broken. The story wasn't meant to go this way, and it began to show.

Wales's fly-half, James Hook, missed a penalty. France, meanwhile, kicked three. A dummy and darting try from scrum-half Mike Phillips brought Wales back into contention, but James missed the conversion. Then Stephen Jones, replacing James, missed another penalty. With just six minutes of the match left and the score lying at Wales 8 – France 9, Wales were awarded yet another penalty. The story, after everything that had happened, could still find the ending for which Wales had hoped.

The penalty was just inside the halfway line, forty-nine metres from the posts, so it was Wales's long-range goal-kicker, twenty-two-year-old Leigh Halfpenny, who stepped up to the mark.

When Leigh was nine, his grandfather started picking him up from his primary school in Pontybrenin to take him for kicking practice on the rugby pitch in Gorseinon. If he was tired, Leigh's grandfather would still persuade his grandson to practise. 'Come on now,' he'd say with a smile. 'Let's get it done, is it?' Towards the end of a session he'd sometimes try to put pressure on him too, telling him, 'One more, is it? But this one's to beat England,' or 'This one's for the final of the World Cup.' As Leigh grew older, he needed little encouragement, practising his kicking every day of the year, including Christmas Day. The England fly-half, Jonny Wilkinson, became his role model. Leigh read all his books and watched all his DVDs just so he could study his hero's kicking technique.

When Leigh was fifteen, he caught the eye of the Neath and Swansea Ospreys academy. But at the age of eighteen the Ospreys dropped him for being too small. Determined to make it in top-level rugby, Leigh embarked on a stringent weights regime, putting himself through sets in which he regularly 'lifted to failure' – until his muscles could no longer work. His parents spent thousands on nutritional supplements. At the age of nineteen, having just been signed for Cardiff Blues, Leigh made his debut for Wales.

Three years later, under the floodlights of Eden Park, Leigh prepared to take the kick for which he'd practised all his life. This was his schoolboy's dream made reality: the penalty that could take his country into its first-ever World Cup Final. After all those hours with his grandfather on the pitch at Gorseinon, after all those years of building himself up, after the pain of the Spała training camps in Poland, the moment he'd envisaged so many times had finally come.

Removing his skullcap Leigh placed the ball on the kicking tee as if it was the last piece in a delicate puzzle. Angling it away from him, he stood and stepped backwards and then to the side. Behind him, at his shoulder, was Neil Jenkins, or 'Jenks', the Wales kicking coach. Jenks, reciting a quiet list of pointers, knew this kick was within Leigh's range. And so did Leigh. In training he'd regularly converted longer kicks than this from inside his own half.

Standing with his knees slightly bent and with his hands rocking rhythmically at his sides, Leigh stared down at the ball in front of him. The roars of the crowd washed around the stadium, rising and falling like waves. Eyeing the posts for a last time he lowered his head and, slowly tipping forward, took a series of quickening steps towards the ball. Planting his left foot firmly beside the tee, Leigh struck the ball hard with his right foot, sudden and sharp, straight towards the posts.

The hands of the Welsh fans at Eden Park immediately rose above their heads. And in the Red Lion in New York, and in the Three Kings in London, and in the Millennium Stadium in Cardiff thousands of other pairs of hands also reached into the air. And rising with them, across the time zones of the world, came a cheer, voiced as one by every Welsh supporter on the planet. The ball was sailing towards the middle of the posts.

But then, instead of building to a crescendo, the cheer began to fade. The raised hands began to fall – in the Red Lion, in the Three Kings, in the Millennium Stadium – coming to rest on the tops of their owners' heads. And that's where they stayed, in an image of despair, as the ball, turning end over end, dropped short of the crossbar by an inch. Leigh had missed the kick.

Five minutes later the match was over, the final score Wales 8 – France 9.

The script was written. Wales had lost.


Skirting the edge of the pitch I walk around the stadium's bowl to the mouth of the player's tunnel and walk up it, the thousands of empty seats diminishing behind me. Once inside, further down the corridor that leads towards the Wales changing rooms, I can make out the eleven dark wooden boards on which every Welsh player's cap number and name is written in gold leaf. The first, in 1881, is James Bevan, an Australian who played for my old club, Abergavenny, and the first captain of Wales. The last is number 1,089, Alex Cuthbert, a young winger who won his first cap here last month when he was twenty-one, just four years after he'd first picked up a rugby ball. Between them, nested in the tight rows at number 430, is my great-great-uncle, Archie Skym. Capped twenty times, Archie was nicknamed 'The Butcher', although at thirteen stone, regardless of being a prop, he'd still be the lightest member of the squad today.

I descend the flight of stairs and pass the silver dragon on the wall again. Pausing to look at it I realise this is the first thing a visiting team will see on a match day. That claw, raised between salute and attack.

Previous World Cups have been catalysts for change for Wales. In the wake of disappointing performances coaches were sacked, new methods adopted, a rash of new players brought into the squad. But the World Cup in New Zealand posed a different question for the national side. Here was a young squad, mostly at the start of their careers, already hitting their stride. They hadn't felt lucky to be in that semi-final, but they had felt unlucky to lose it. So the question it posed to Wales was no longer one of change, but of promise. In both senses of the word.

Could Wales fulfil the promise they'd shown? And could they keep the promise they'd apparently made by playing so well at the highest level? Could they return to Europe and stamp their mark on northern-hemisphere rugby, not just by winning the coming Six Nations tournament, but by winning all five of their matches to secure a third Welsh Grand Slam in eight seasons? Only two other generations of Welsh players had ever won three Grand Slams: between 1905 and 1911, and between 1971 and 1978. Could Warren Gatland's youngsters, with the majority of their international playing days still ahead of them, be the third golden generation of Welsh rugby? Ever since their semi-final defeat to France, this has been the question on the lips of Welsh supporters and, although unspoken, in the minds of the Welsh players too.

As I leave the stadium, nodding to Gwyn through the double plate glass of his security lodge, I know there's no way of knowing the answer. Rugby's script is written in the moment. Even the players in the squad do not know yet who will play in those five matches. Or which of them out celebrating tonight, as yet uncapped, might see their names added in gold leaf to those dark wooden boards. The only certainty is that those five matches will happen and that they will be won or not, each result leaving in its wake either a trail of disappointment or jubilation, celebration or mourning. 'It's either the wedding game or the funeral game with us,' 'Thumper' Phillips, the Wales team manager, once said to me from behind his desk at the Vale. 'Nothing in between.'

Two of those five matches will be played away, against Ireland in Dublin and England at Twickenham. The other three will be played here, on the meadow and rye grass of the Millennium Stadium. First against Scotland, then Italy, and then, in Wales's last match of the tournament, on 17 March at 2.45 p.m., France. Whether or not that last game will also be a Grand Slam decider for Wales will depend on the balance of the scorelines of the preceding matches, each of them a challenge in its own right, in which the Welsh players will push their bodies to the limit in their attempts to tip the scales of those scorelines in their favour.

5 February

Ireland 21 – Wales 23

## 12 February

Wales 27 – Scotland 13

25 February

England 12 – Wales 19

10 March

Wales 24 – Italy 3

Former Wales captain Mervyn Davies has died following a battle with cancer. He was 65.

Known universally as 'Merv the Swerve' the number eight won a total of 38 caps for Wales and went on two victorious British and Irish Lions tours in 1971 and 1974.

Davies won two Grand Slams with Wales and three Triple Crowns. Davies was handed the captaincy of Wales in 1975 and skippered the side to the Five Nations Championship in the same year, and the Grand Slam the following season.

At 6ft 3in, Davies sometimes appeared ungainly on the field, but that belied his strength in the maul. He also had an uncanny sense of anticipation, allowing him to get to the breakdown first – and his height made him useful in the line-out.

In a poll of Welsh rugby fans in 2002, Davies was voted greatest Welsh captain and greatest Welsh number eight.

# Now and Then

What might have been and what has been
Point to one end, which is always present.
T. S. Eliot, 'Burnt Norton'

There are moments in history
when a nation becomes a stadium.
When a country's gaze and speech
tightens in one direction.

When a population leans, from sofas,
pub stools, in village halls, to watch.
Or strains to listen at the sides of roads,
or in tractor cabs in silent fields.

There are moments when the many,
through the few, become one.

A faithful but demanding tribe,
hungry for a win but also more.
For beauty as well as strength,
for art as well as war.

But romance, history, fervour,
are the privilege of watchers only.
For the men who must do,
though fuelled by the colour of the jersey,

the feathers on their chest, there can be no past
or future when, but only now.

For them those eighty tightening minutes
will be an ever-living present
composed of the angle of their runs,
the timing of cross kicks, the learned set piece

that fires the line to light the match.
It will be the focused practice
of what their bodies have learnt on the training pitch.
The thousands of hours of solitary pain,

the sacrifice that has led them,
and them alone, to this –

A nation sharing a pulse
as the clock counts up to the final whistle
when now becomes then. The moment,
whichever way it falls, cast forever,

and theirs to carry for the rest of their lives
until, like those who've passed through
this crucible before, they too will join
the soil, the *tir,* the *pridd* of this land

they were prepared to suffer for.

# GAME DAY

## Wales vs France, 17 March 2012

### 6 a.m.

Michael, a wiry seventy-five-year-old from Barry Island, gives Gwyn a wave as he enters the stadium. Gwyn doesn't need to check his pass. Michael, white-haired, bespectacled, has been working as a volunteer with the ground staff here for years. And every match day he does this, walking in on his own at 6 a.m.

Gwyn follows Michael on the CCTV monitor as he makes his way past the players' entrance and round a corner towards the service areas. Michael is the only person on Gwyn's quartered screen, his small body marooned in an expanse of angled, unpainted concrete, as if he's walking through an architecture built for a species more gigantic than human.

Following the coach-wide passageway, two storeys high, Michael passes through the groundsman's storage supplies. Piles of fertiliser and nutrients, Kioti tractors, frames for the growing lights, spools of orange rope all crowd and gather at the walls. Three racing-green Dennis pedestrian cylinder mowers are parked in a row, clumps of grass like chewed cud collected in their barrels.

Everything around Michael is on a massive scale, like the sound stage of a film studio stacked with the sets of an epic.

As Michael enters a room on his left, however, everything is suddenly more intimate. With the single swing of a door, the stadium's vocabulary of event is translated into a more domestic dialect. A round wooden table at the centre of the room is scattered with newspapers, four chairs around it: three plastic uprights and one double-sized ox-blood leather Chesterfield. Against the wall another, smaller table is crowded with mugs, teabags, coffee jars, a kettle and a small fridge. Apart from one life-size poster of Katherine Jenkins wearing a sequinned dress, the walls are covered exclusively with A4 photographs of the stadium's pitch, each of them labelled with a year and the name of Wales's opponents on that day:

2007 – Ireland
2009 – England
2011 – Argentina

In each photograph the pattern mown into the grass is different: checkered, long and short rectangles, stripes, diamonds in the dead-ball area.

This is the groundsman's office, which Michael shares with Lee, the head groundsman, and Craig, his assistant from John O'Groats. Lee and Craig call the photographs on the walls their 'pitch porn': a record of every pattern they've ever cut into the grass of the national ground, each one the result of considered discussion around the wooden table, sketches on envelopes, the laying of miles and miles of orange guide string and a strict regime of cutting and double cutting.

'I doubt no one else ever notices,' Craig once told Michael in his Scottish accent. ''Cept for us. And our wives, when they see it on tha telly.'

The high-backed ox-blood Chesterfield belongs to Craig, the two gentle depressions in its seat marking the outline of his buttocks. He bought the chair via fatfingers.com, a website that lists misspellings on eBay. He wanted it for his home in Cardiff, only realising it was double-sized when he went to collect it. Stadium-sized.

'My wife was'na havin' it in the house,' he explained to Lee when he turned up with it at the groundsman's office. 'So I thaw I'd bring it here instead.'

Under the unblinking smile of Katherine Jenkins, Michael makes a cup of tea, stirring in a spoonful of sugar before taking his mug back out into the passageway and up into the stadium's bowl. He enters pitch-side via the 'Dragon's Mouth', a hydraulic ramp that opens and closes like a set of massive jaws.

The stadium's roof is open, but only by a metre. A slim line of early daylight falls directly onto the halfway line. Despite a forecast of rain, the French coach, Philippe Saint-André, has asked for the retractable roof to be opened. Warren Gatland, who would rather it stayed closed, joked at a press conference a few days earlier that perhaps when they tried to open it, the mechanism would fail and the roof would have to remain shut. This morning, when staff began opening the roof, the mechanism broke, leaving just this hairline of light falling onto the pitch.

Michael stands at the north-east corner and sips his tea. When he was younger, it was football, not rugby, that was his game. In his twenties he even won a couple of Welsh caps. After his playing days were over, he got a job as a groundsman at a cricket club, and while he was there cricket became his focus. Having retired from the club, he was working as a gardener at a hotel in Cardiff when, six years ago, Lee's predecessor asked him if he'd like to come and help out at the Millennium Stadium. Ever since, rugby and this stadium have occupied Michael's interest.

Holding his mug in both hands, Michael looks out over the pitch. The grass is patterned in even rectangles of pale green and deep emerald. It has been cut, cleared of feathers from the young birds moulting in the roof, then cut again. The whitewash of the touchlines, trylines, twenty-two-metre, ten-metre, dead-ball and halfway lines has been replenished. Michael himself has trimmed the grass round each set of posts with a pair of scissors. The pitch is ready.

Michael takes a deep breath and begins to feel the sensation he always feels when he comes in this early on a match day welling in his chest: 'A deep fucking sadness.' He gives the pitch a nod – part approval, part acceptance – then takes another sip of tea before starting his customary lap of the stadium. As he walks, the sadness continues to grow through him, like a blush of melancholy. 'I don't knows why,' he says when asked about it. 'It just does. There's not another soul in the place, but I just feels so fucking sad. 'Cos it's all over, I suppose. Until we start again.'

No one else spends as much time on the grass of the national pitch as Lee, Craig and Michael. Everyone feels ownership over it: Roger Lewis, the chief executive of the WRU; the members of the WRU board; Gerry, the stadium manager; the fans; and, of course, the Wales coaches and players. But if ownership were measured in time, then Michael, Lee and Craig could make a better claim than most. Every time Lee and Craig double-cut the grass it's a twelve-mile walk if working on their own, or six miles each if working together. Between them they've seen hundreds of players pass across the turf. Their days start early, around 7 a.m., and on the eve of a match they'll often be giving the pitch its final cut well into the night. As they work, pushing the mowers under the floodlights at a determined, steady pace, they both listen to Radio 2 on their headphones. Sometimes they'll text in a request – 'for the groundsmen working on the Millennium Stadium'. If the song is played, they'll raise a silent fist to each other across the empty pitch, before dropping their eyes to the turf again to continue their mowing, making sure to only ever 'walk down the light and never the dark', so as not to disturb their patterns of pale- and deep-green grass.

Michael pauses at the southern end of the pitch, the part of the stadium Lee and Craig call the 'Bat-Cave'. Whatever the time of year, from row four back this portion of the ground never gets any sunlight. This is the turf that needs the most attention and the greatest amount of time under the growing lights. A succession of wheeling scrums in this part of the pitch can cause Lee and Craig, and therefore their wives, sleepless nights.

Facing Michael at the other end of the stadium is an Under Armour advertising banner. As long as several buses, it hangs from the roof behind the raked seating of the North Stand. The torsos and arms of five Welsh players fill its canvas, their red, three-feathered shirts stretched tight across their chests and biceps. At one time the banner used to show the players' heads too, but now it's been cropped, cutting them off at the neck. The turnover in the squad became too rapid and the scale of the image too expensive to recreate.

A team is both eternal and ephemeral, its members forever changing. As Warren Gatland often reminds his young squad, they're only borrowing the red shirt of Wales. Injury or another player rising through the ranks can be just around the corner. So the shirt is only borrowing them too. And that's what the cropped banner seems to say. You will borrow the shirt, and the shirt will borrow you, but only the shirt and the team will remain. You who fill out both are just passing through. *Yesterday*, as the banner in the Barn never lets the squad forget, *is in the past.*

## 6.30 a.m.

The eighty minutes of today's match, though, are still in the future, and as Michael completes his lap of the stadium, this is what the men who'll wear those red shirts today are thinking about as they wake up. It is still early, but as Michael leaves the stadium's bowl by the Dragon's Mouth, as he takes his growing sadness back to Barry, thinking, 'Sod this, I'm off home for some breakfast,' the Welsh players, twelve miles west in their shared rooms at the Vale Resort in Pontyclun, are already stirring. Their minds will have woken before their bodies, occupied with thinking about the day's events. Their stomachs are light with nerves. Those who asked Prof. John, the team doctor, for a sleeping pill to get them through the night are still asleep. But those who didn't are already waking and, therefore, from the second they open their eyes, preparing.

Their captain, Sam Warburton, wakes up thinking of food. Not the taste of it, but the value of it. Food as fuel. This will be his main concern for the rest of the day until he boards the team bus for the journey into the city centre. How to make sure his body has the calories it needs for the exertion ahead? As he lies in his bed he visualises his body as an empty tank, filling through the day's three meals before the match so that, at kick-off, he will be ready. But to be ready he has to keep that food inside his system, and on a match day that can be a challenge in itself. Sam wants the food, needs the food, but his nerves often kill his appetite and make his stomach unpredictable. More than once he's coughed in the shower before a game only to find himself following through and vomiting up the pre-match meal. If that happens, Sam, panicked, will make straight for the team room to drink a protein shake and eat a banana. Although he doesn't want solids inside him at kick-off, just their nutritional resonance, he knows he needs the fuel. And so he will eat, to give his body and the team he captains the best chance of coming through those eighty minutes on top.

Down the corridor from the room Sam shares with Dan Lydiate, his playing partner at blindside flanker, the team's centres, Jonathan Davies and Jamie Roberts, are also rooming together. On international days, other than when eating Jonathan would usually sleep and nap through the hours in the build-up to a match. But today is no ordinary match and the prospect of what lies ahead will keep him awake for the rest of the morning and afternoon.

For the last two months the words 'Grand Slam' have rarely been spoken in the Welsh camp, although journalists at the ever-growing press conferences have been using the phrase with increasing regularity. The Welsh newspapers, with typical enthusiasm, began seeding the phrase in their articles after the team's first win over Ireland. But the Welsh players and coaches have always remained focused on the next game in the competition, rather than the potential prize at its end. For a squad in camp, expectation and aspiration are volatile fuels, essential but combustible. Given too much of an airing they'll easily explode the very potency that brings a team success. Privately, though, the thought of winning a Grand Slam has never been far from the thoughts of the Welsh squad. From the moment Wales lost to France in the World Cup, Sam, not usually a superstitious man, acknowledged a strong intuition that Wales 'deserved something good to happen' in the coming Six Nations. After another rehab and conditioning week of cold-weather training at Gdansk in Poland, the squad entered the tournament with the belief that they were just too good to fail. But they were also realistic. Sport can be cruel, and rugby more cruel than most. Key World Cup players such as Alun Wyn Jones and Gethin Jenkins were still injured, as was the hooker and former captain Matthew Rees. Nothing could be taken for granted. Which is why, as with each win Grand Slam fever infected more and more of Wales, the Welsh camp itself has remained an island of calm within the country.

Over the course of the tournament the players and coaches training at the Vale have been subjected to an ever-tightening focus of attention. Since last week's victory over Italy, today's match against France has dominated the national conversation. At service stations as you fuel your car, in cafes, pubs, restaurants, staffrooms and offices, schools and hospitals, wherever you'll have gone in Wales for the past week you will have heard aspects of the coming match being endlessly dissected and examined. Anticipation is the lifeblood of the sports fan. This morning, on the brink of a possible third Grand Slam in eight years, there are few in Wales who have not been anticipating today's match and, for this week at least, not become fans.

And yet despite this overheated cauldron of obsession, the Welsh camp at the Vale – the Castle training pitch, the gyms, the team room, the Barn – has somehow managed to maintain its lower operating temperature. For the last two months, on entering its environment players and coaches alike have felt a palpable expansion of the chest and mind, as if it's here, at the very eye of the storm, where they can think and breathe most clearly, where they can feel most at home.

Until this week. Over the last six days the seal on the Vale's vacuum has begun to leak. The press conferences have continued to grow, with journalists arriving from France, Italy, Argentina. At each session a forest of camera tripods jostle for position, the Dictaphones on the top table multiplying like cells dividing.

The public have followed the press too, with fans, families and sponsors all converging on the Vale in the hope of meeting, or just seeing, one of Wales's prospective Grand Slam champions. The players are the same men who started this campaign just six weeks ago, but already success has gilded each of them with the blessing and the curse of being 'a child o' the time'.

Like many of the squad, Jonathan Davies has attempted to escape the mounting pressure and protect his time away from training. He's begun using the service elevators and back entrances of the hotel, and hasn't read or listened to any of the press coverage of the match. The atmosphere at the Vale, he says, has become 'surreal'. But at the same time it's been impossible to avoid the thought of what a win against France today would mean. Over the last few days, as he and Jamie have discussed game plans and tactics in their room, they've also allowed themselves, for the first time, to speak those two words openly – 'Grand Slam'. Not as an inevitability, but as a whispered possibility. With the other four matches of the campaign successfully behind them, they've begun to imagine what the wake of a fifth victory might look like. What would Wales look like if, through the alchemy of today's match, they could transfigure the current ore of expectation into the precious metal of celebration?

For Jamie, who debuted for Wales against Scotland during their Grand Slam campaign in 2008, his projection of that possible future is conjured upon the taste of experience. For three of the older players in the squad – Ryan Jones, Gethin Jenkins and Adam Jones – a win would mark their third Grand Slam each and see them join a select group of just three other Welsh players who've achieved the same. But for Jonathan and the majority of this young squad this would be their first experience of a Grand Slam. The squad's younger players are all in unfamiliar territory, on the brink of realising a childhood dream which none of them, until these last few days, had dared to think could ever come true.

Now just twenty-three, Jonathan was a spectator in the stands at Wales's last two Grand Slams, in 2005 and 2008. When he was growing up in west Wales, he remembers it being an 'unwritten rule' that every Welsh boy would try to play rugby at some point in their life. Jonathan was just five years old when he answered that national stipulation, picking up his first rugby ball at Bancyfelin Primary School, the same school where Mike Phillips, Wales's scrum-half today, began his playing days. Jonathan played as a junior for St Clears, then, when the side disbanded, for Whitland, before, at the age of fifteen, moving on to the Scarlets academy. It was, though, a summer of fitness training with the father of one of his brother's friends, Jeff Stephenson, that Jonathan cites as the crucial turning point of his teenage years. Training with Jeff over those summer weeks turned him from a 'chubby kid' into what he describes as 'more of a physical presence'. As he got bigger, so his position altered, moving down the line from scrum-half, to outside-half, to centre.

Throughout his youth Jonathan always considered himself as one of the bigger backs in the game, and he'd have been right to think so. Just listening to his voice without seeing him is enough to give you an idea of his size. Assured and gravelled it seems to rise from a deep Welsh quarry, resonant with his sixteen stone three pounds of weight. But size is relative, and in this current Welsh team Jonathan has come to think of himself as being on the smaller side. Of the six other men in the Welsh backline today three are taller and heavier than him, including his room-mate in the bed next to him this morning, Jamie Roberts, who at six foot four and seventeen stone four pounds still isn't the biggest back in the squad.

There was a time when the positions in a rugby-union team catered for a broad spectrum of body shapes: from the full-sail bellies of the props and the tall, cross-beam-shouldered locks, to the shorter, terrier-like scrum-halves and the more slender full-backs and wings. In Wales particularly this pattern resonated with an echo of the country's class and economic hierarchy: the claustrophobic, bowed, scrummaging forwards working at the coalface of a match to win possession for the more individually minded backs, who using their greater freedom of movement and expression would exploit the forwards' efforts, cashing in with a profit of tries and conversions.

In Wales these backline entrepreneurs were traditionally the smaller men on the pitch, quick and visionary with game-changing side-steps and tackle-defying low centres of gravity. Their body shapes were those of the Welsh soldiers observed by Wilfred Owen in the trenches of the First World War, the 'stocky mountain men' of his ancestry whose same attributes of quickness and shorter stature made them, in the eyes of the poet, good infantry-men as well as good backs.

Though written into the game as early as the 1900s, this Welsh signature of backline play became epitomised in the great teams of the 1970s, in the form of Barry John, Gareth Edwards, J. P. R. Williams, Phil Bennett and Gerald Davies. Of these it was perhaps Gerald Davies who made the most from the tension drawn between the contrasting scales of his physicality and his penetration on the field. Although slight of build, Gerald could tear opposing teams apart, in more than one match scoring every time he touched the ball. His defining skills – a quickness of reaction, a side-step of both feet at full speed, his spatial reading of the game – were all products of his smaller stature. Carwyn James has written how Gerald developed the 'instincts of a forest animal', exploiting a survivalist's fear to keep him out of harm's way and, therefore, the hands of the opposition. 'Fear', James writes, 'is an important element in the make-up of such a player.'

The resulting style of rugby played by Gerald rang true against the dominant notes of Welsh support – a demand for beauty as well as brutality, a celebration of the small winning over the big. It's a playing style that's been kept alive by a succession of smaller backs, most recently in the quickstep feet of Shane Williams, the diminutive winger who, having scored more tries than any other Welshman, retired in December with yet another try against Australia, followed by a gymnast's farewell somersault. But while Gerald's body shape remained largely unchanged throughout his playing days, Shane's increasingly showed the pressure of the times. Compared to his younger self, the Shane who accepted the crowd's applause after that somersault was almost two stone heavier than the Shane who first took the field for Wales. His neck was thicker, his arms pushed wider by bulked-up lats, his shoulders were piled higher and his chest and biceps were tight with new muscle. The change in Shane's body was a sign of what was to come for Wales. He still scored tries through flexibility and speed, but to stay in the modern game he had to be able to take and give the hits too.

Ever since rugby union turned professional, the body shape and contribution of its players have become more uniform. While each position still has its specialism, the breadth of an individual's requirements in top-flight rugby have also grown. Forwards are now expected to move quickly around the field and handle like a back. In turn, the backs are expected to scavenge at the turn-over and put their shoulder to the rucks or mauls. And everyone tackles. Where Barry John could once claim to his captain 'tackling isn't in my contract' as he ran out for the Grand Slam match against France in 1971, Wales's number ten facing the French today, Rhys Priestland, will more than likely make shuddering tackles well into double figures.

Wales's response to the increased physicality in the game has been to enter a period of gigantism. On the eve of the Scottish match the *Guardian*, reflecting on Wales's win in Dublin the week before, published an illustrated comparison of the backlines of four international teams: Wales, England, New Zealand and South Africa. The pictures of twenty-eight big men ranged across two pages of the paper. But for the first time ever, and against the grain of Welsh tradition, none of the other backlines was bigger than the Welsh, who stood on average two inches taller and almost a stone heavier. For their Six Nations opponents these statistics were all the more imposing because of what the rugby world had witnessed the previous weekend at the Aviva Stadium in Dublin: a backline of young Welsh giants, yet still possessed with the skills and speed of those men who'd worn the same numbers on their backs in the 1970s.

Many of those ex-Welsh players had travelled to Dublin to watch that opening match against Ireland, including Gerald Davies, who now writes on rugby for *The Times*. As a lover of T. S. Eliot's poetry, Gerald had a CD of *The Four Quartets* in his car when he drove to the airport that weekend. As he listened to 'East Coker' on that drive, Gerald would have heard the poem's opening line – *In my beginning is my end*. It's a line which this morning, as the Welsh players at the Vale stir and wake in their beds, rings truer than ever in relation to that opening match against Ireland. An opening match which not only set the tone for Wales's tournament, but also laid the stones for today's Grand Slam decider against France.

The Welsh team flew to Ireland across a snow-dusted Wales and a corrugated sea, both suitable preparations for the frosty, rough-edged reception waiting for them in Dublin. The talk on the city's streets and in the press was of World Cup revenge. Not for Wales's loss to France, but for Ireland's loss to Wales. Having outmuscled Australia, Ireland went on to the quarter-finals, only to be out-thought by a tactically astute Wales. As a reminder of that defeat, on the morning of the match the Irish papers carried a photograph of a jubilant Mike Phillips leaping into the air, his fist clenched, against a backdrop of bowed heads in green shirts. The Celtic tiger was still smarting and now, it was felt, on a cold Sunday in February, with every second mannequin on Grafton Street wearing one of those green shirts and the gulls skating across a frozen St Stephen's pond, was the time to bite back.

There were other undercurrents of tension pulling at the Irish game too. Ten years ago the Irish Rugby Union had sacked Warren Gatland and replaced him with his assistant coach, Eddie O'Sullivan. In the wake of the World Cup both teams were injury-hit, but with a strong record of home wins against Wales, recent club victories in Europe and an undefeated run at their new stadium the Irish, even without their talismanic captain Brian O'Driscoll, were the bookies' favourites. Wales, meanwhile, had followed their World Cup loss to France with two more straight defeats, both against Australia. With these games in mind Austin Healey, the ex-England international, delivered a forecast shared by many commentators:

> The Irish are flying; they've got three teams through to the quarter-finals of the Heineken Cup and have a strong squad. I'm expecting Ireland to beat Wales by at least 14 points. Put me on the spot and I'd say 27–9 because the Irish players have been doing so well in Europe. It will be pretty tough for Wales. I'm predicting they will finish fourth in the Six Nations table with only two wins, against Scotland and Italy.

Psychologically, if not physically, every international rugby match begins weeks before the kick-off. For the Irish game, despite predictions like Healey's, Wales had won this pre-match contest before they'd even landed in Dublin. The underdog label suited them. The squad would rather fight for a win from underneath than protect a perceived advantage from above. With a typical deftness of touch Warren had postponed his own team announcement until after Ireland had shown their hand, having already seeded certain ideas in the minds of the Irish selectors. Photographs of Jamie Roberts sitting on the sidelines at training had been printed in the papers, suggesting the big Welsh centre wasn't yet match fit. Jamie went on to have what he later described as 'one of his best days ever in a Welsh shirt'.

However well Wales contested the build-up to the match, the game itself remained a massive challenge. A vengeful Ireland at home is a daunting prospect for any team. Without the retired Shane Williams Wales were fielding an untried new wing pairing of George North and Alex Cuthbert, as well as a vastly altered pack from the World Cup, with the towering Ian Evans back after three years of injury and the rookie Rhys Gill coming in at loose head to replace the veteran Gethin Jenkins. The question of promise posed to Wales in the wake of their World Cup defeat suddenly looked like a significantly harder one to answer.

For Jonathan Davies the Ireland match presented a more personal challenge. On the Thursday before the game his grandfather died, and Jonathan had to carry this loss with him across the Irish Sea and into the stadium that Sunday afternoon. Singing the national anthem when you're about to play for Wales is emotional for any player; a moment when the compression of the occasion focuses a player's thoughts upon certain individuals in their life. The lyrics may be of nationhood – '*Mae hen wlad fy nhadau yn annwyl i mi*' ('The land of my fathers which is dear to me') – but in the minds of the young men singing them those lyrics often evoke people more than a place: the families, wives, girlfriends, parents and grandparents who over the years have helped make this moment possible for them, and whose own dreams, by playing for Wales that day, they are making come true.

For Jonathan, singing the anthem in Dublin was almost too much. Intensified through the prism of his grandfather's death, it was all he could do to contain himself and gather his thoughts for the game ahead. The resonance of that emotional intensity, however, would remain with him for the next eighty minutes, and never more so than when, just fifteen minutes after singing the anthem, he gathered a sweetly timed offload from Rhys Priestland and crossed to score Wales's first try of the match. As Jonathan walked back from the Irish tryline he flicked his eyes skyward, then kissed the ball with which he'd just scored before raising it, briefly, in salute. He went on to follow that first try with another in the second half, scored that cold Sunday, like the first, for his grandfather as well as for Wales.

In the end everything worked out for Wales that day. The match was painfully close, at times no more than an inch or a second from being lost, and it was far from perfect. For ten minutes, when Bradley Davies was sinbinned, Wales once again found themselves playing with fourteen men. Rhys Priestland squandered eight points in missed penalties and conversions. But despite these setbacks Wales displayed a new strain of mental and physical toughness for the full eighty minutes. For eighty minutes they brought their memories of Spała and Gdansk to the

Aviva pitch and they used them, at the very last moment, to win against a home side on form and bent on revenge.

Winning in sport is often about repetition; about trying to recreate that elusive blend of preparation, discipline, rhythm and instinct. Routine, though never the key on its own, is often the path teams and individuals choose to bring themselves closer to that winning recipe. Today, in the eight hours before the match against France, the Welsh players waking in their beds at the Vale will each follow an interwoven pattern of individual and squad routines. Jonathan Davies, wanting to avoid a 'dullness of the eyes', will choose not to watch TV or play any computer games. Sam Warburton, when not focusing on fuelling his body, will isolate himself. Lloyd Williams, the young scrum-half, will begin a new book. Adam Jones, the tight-head prop, will call his wife and listen to the sounds of his new baby daughter on the phone.

Adam, or 'Bomb' as he is known within the squad, is one of the team's better-known faces. Already a veteran of two Grand Slams, his distinctive mop of dark curls has earned him yet another moniker in public. When he played alongside another similarly hirsute prop, Duncan Jones, the pair became known as Wales's 'Hair Bears'. It's an appearance which also caught the eye of Boris Johnson, the mayor of London, who once claimed Adam as his favourite athlete, both because he'd played prop himself and because he said Adam reminded him of 'Cro-Magnon man'. Before Adam's last match against France at the World Cup, Boris even phoned his hotel room to wish him good luck, which was, Adam admits in his quick Breconshire accent, 'a very, very surreal moment'.

Within rugby, Adam is as well known for the quality of his scrummaging and the depth of his knowledge as for his haircut. The bar he's set at tight head is so high it's now the one position in the squad where Wales struggle to find equivalent cover. Over the last few years he's brought his weight down from twenty-three stone to closer to nine-teen, lifting his levels of fitness to keep pace with the modern game. Amenable and gentle off the field, with a quick sense of self-deprecating humour, Adam doesn't think of himself as 'a very confrontational bloke'. And yet during a match he's often the epitome of the word, whether packing down to take on an opposition front row or throwing himself into tackles, his long hair flying about his head a visual register of the force he's put into the impact.

In France the front row is as iconic among rugby fans as the outside-half is in Wales. The French pride themselves on their scrummaging ability, on their tradition of dominating opposing packs. So Adam knows today will be another hard day at the office, and that he'll need to protect his right shoulder to avoid being shunted by the French. But at least he's back with his British Lions teammates, Matthew Rees and Gethin Jenkins, both recovered from injury. Between the three of them they present a front line of massive experience; a vanguard of hundreds of international hours behind which the team's younger backline will hopefully be able to go to work.

Adam, like all the squad, will go for a 'primer' today. Not that long ago these didn't exist, with teams doing all their physical preparation at the stadium. For several years they consisted of no more than a weights session. Today, although many players will still use weights to stimulate their nervous systems, to give their bodies a match-day sensation of tightness, the primer is more individually focused. Under the instruction of Adam Beard, Wales's head of physical performance, the primer is now about responding to the specific needs of that player on that day. Some will stretch existing tension in certain muscle groups. Others will work on co-ordination skills, sharpen reaction times. The backs will also walk through their moves, while the forwards will walk through their line-out drills, laying down the rhythms of each call in their muscle memories. For Leigh Halfpenny, once again today's long-range goal-kicker, his primer will be to do what he's done a thousand times before: go down to the Castle training pitch and practise his kicks with Jenks. And because this is a match day he'll do this not just for the kicking itself, but also 'to get a feel for the day': the quality and strength of the wind, the weight of the weather, the taste of the light.

Roger Lewis, the chief executive of the Welsh Rugby Union, stands on the edge of the Millennium Stadium pitch, bathed in the warm light of a camera crew. Dressed in a grey suit, red WRU tie and red scarf, he is giving an interview to the BBC. Beside him the Blims, a five-man band from Bridgend, are warming up to play their Grand Slam song, 'Sidesteps and Sideburns', which over the past week has become a YouTube hit. They wear the red and white striped scarves of the 1970s, and the lead singer has thick sideburns reminiscent of the era. Even when celebrating today's team, most of whom were born in the late 1980s, Welsh rugby's stubborn memories of the 1970s still persist, as if support of a contemporary squad will always be tainted by comparison.

The camera turns towards the Blims, and they begin to play.

A long time ago before I was born we once had a
    team that was always adored,
with sidesteps and sideburns and Grand Slams
    galore,
our magical boys wrote their names in folklore.

The BBC broadcast shows live on the big screens hanging from the North and South Stands, briefly committing the Blims to a diminishing hall of mirrors as they appear on a screen within a screen within a screen. Roger looks on, smiling, knowing that today his stadium and his team are at the centre of the centre.

Roger is fifty-eight years old, but with his neatly parted brown hair, trim figure and senator's smile he looks fifteen years younger. Having studied music composition and worked as a composer and musician, Roger came to the WRU in 2006 via executive positions at Radio 1, Classic FM, EMI and Decca. Although now firmly ensconced in rugby, he sometimes feels as if on a match day his two worlds still meet in this stadium, the teams like orchestras, the game a concert and the referee the conductor. Music and rugby come together at Roger's home in St Hilary too, where he'll often work into the night on his laptop beside the fire, deep in WRU business but always accompanied by one of the thousands of CDs from his room-sized library next door.

This morning marks the apex of Roger's time with the WRU. When he first joined the organisation, it was struggling, on and off the pitch. In 2010, after a difficult season, he was questioned both privately and publicly about the wisdom of extending Warren Gatland's contract as Wales head coach. Today, though, having reduced the organisation's debt, opened up new revenue streams, secured Warren until after the 2015 World Cup and signed new sponsorship and broadcast deals, he will watch as Wales make a bid for their third Grand Slam in eight years. There are still issues. Regional rugby is fighting to keep its head above water, and many in the game are looking to Roger and the WRU to throw it a lifeline. There have been accusations that the national game is thriving at the expense of local rugby. There are always others who would do things differently. But today, just a year after those doubts about his decision-making were expressed, Roger is enjoying, for a few hours at least, being at the helm of the WRU when the country is febrile with talk of a third golden generation of Welsh rugby.

In his own way, like the players and the coaches he employs Roger is a winner who thrives on the hit of success. Ruthless in pursuit of his ideas and a shrewd judge of character, he's a man unafraid to explore the visionary and the experimental. Driven by a desire to fly 'at great heights', he's moved swiftly through the higher echelons of the music and broadcasting industries. And yet, despite his current position and the depth of his past experience, there is still something permanently boyish about Roger, as if Just William had suddenly woken to find himself a successful executive, still effervescent with the surprise of his new found powers in the grown up world.

Behind Roger the stadium's roof is still only open by a metre. All around him the building is being prepared. PR women high-heel down the players' tunnel, phones to their ears, clipboards balanced like babies at their hips. The suited event managers speak to each other through headsets, while cameramen lay looping armfuls of cables and the sponsor's logos are painted onto the pitch. Thousands of folding seats click and tut from high in the stands as teams of cleaners move through the aisles and rows. Deeper within the building the staff of the Barry John and Gareth Edwards bars on level three are connecting their beer barrels and checking their pumps.

Back home in Barry, meanwhile, Michael, having finished his breakfast, sits in his favourite armchair and turns on the TV. The Blims appear on the screen, playing and singing their song.

> And we'll all hold hands and drink to each other's
> good health,
> And we'll all hold hands and thank the Lord we're
> born Welsh,
> And the more we drink the more we'll sing *Calon*
> *Lan*,
> And we all hope Wales win the Grand Slam.

Michael watches, another cup of tea in his hand, admiring the colour and pattern of the pitch on which the band are playing, the neatness of the grass around the posts.

If Jonathan Davies laid the foundation for Wales's victory against Ireland, it was Leigh Halfpenny who sealed it by kicking a winning penalty in the dying seconds of the match. Just moments before that penalty was awarded it looked as if Eliot's line – *In my beginning is my end* – would have a purely negative resonance for Wales, rather than the positive one it does today. A dead leg meant Sam Warburton didn't come back in the second half, leaving Ryan Jones to step into the breach as captain. Bradley Davies's sixty-fourth-minute sin-binning for dropping his opposite number in an off-the-ball tussle not only evoked the spectre of Sam's World Cup red card, but once again reduced the team to fourteen men. With only four minutes of the match remaining, George North resurrected Welsh hopes by bowling over two Irish defenders to score in the corner. But then Leigh, having taken over kicking duties from Rhys Priestland, missed the conversion, leaving the scoreline of Ireland 21 – Wales 20 also looking like the final result.

But then, as if the gods of rugby were possessed of a perverted love of symmetry, another tip tackle, this time by Ireland's Stephen Ferris on Ian 'Ianto' Evans, opened up a last window of opportunity for Wales, acknowledged by Ianto's grateful ruffle of Ferris's skullcap as he got back to his feet. The penalty was thirty-five metres out and just to the right of the Irish posts. Ryan asked the referee, Wayne Barnes, how much time was left on the clock. His answer was picked up by the TV mikes and broadcast around the world. 'Five zero,' Barnes said. 'Fifty seconds.'

As Leigh angled the ball onto the kicking tee he found himself in the same position as in the final minutes against France at the World Cup in New Zealand: just five steps and one kick from victory or defeat, success or failure, wedding or funeral. Had Wales's World Cup experience made them weaker or stronger? Could Leigh, with one kick, help Wales come true on the promise they'd shown?

When Leigh had missed that kick in Eden Park, his grandfather, the man who'd first taken him to practise in Gorseinon when he was nine, had been watching from half a world away. For this kick in Dublin he was watching again, but this time from within the stands of the same ground, feeling the Aviva's part-arena, part-conservatory atmosphere draw in tight as his grandson stood up from the kicking tee, stabbed the turf with the toe of each boot and began stepping backwards from the ball.

The voice of the crowd fell. A few isolated boos and jeers resounded against the stadium's glass waves, but most of the 55,000 spectators just watched, silent and tense. The last eighty minutes had taken their toll on everyone. Once in position Leigh took a deep breath, his hands swinging at his sides, and looked up at the posts. The noise of the crowd was building again. Whistles, shouts, jeers. The Irish players were lined up under the crossbar, steam rising from their shoulders. His Welsh teammates were standing down the field behind him, their chests rising and falling with heavy breaths. Closer to him, a few metres off his right shoulder, stood Jenks, quietly reciting the same liturgy of technique that he repeats for every kick Leigh takes.

'Keep upright.'

'Not too fast.'

'Make good contact.'

'Follow through.'

Listening to Jenks's voice, Leigh looked down at the ball and located his point of contact. Ever since the kick he'd missed in the semi-final of the World Cup he'd thought about this moment. And every time he had, he'd made the same promise to himself. A promise that if he was ever given the opportunity to kick a winning goal for Wales again, he'd nail it. That he wouldn't ever let what happened at the World Cup happen again. That there was no way he would let the ball fall short. That he wouldn't just kick it, but would kick it as hard as he could.

Taking another deep breath Leigh stared down at the ball, Jenks's voice becoming ever more distant as he tipped his weight forward and began his run-up:

'Keep upright.'

'Not too fast.'

'Make good contact.'

'Follow through.'

*Follow through.*

Leigh has been training with Jenks ever since the ex-Wales and British Lions fly-half came to Swansea to run a kicking session for the Ospreys academy. Leigh was just sixteen at the time and 'nervous as hell' about meeting Wales's greatest-ever kicker. But his grandfather recognised that the session marked the next step in his grandson's career. 'The apprenticeship's over now, boy,' he told Leigh that day. 'I've taken you as far as I can. You're with the main man now.'

As Jenks talks Leigh through his practice kicks on the Castle pitch this morning, a clear sky burning off the river mist, he does not necessarily look like 'the main man' or, some would say, like a rugby player at all. As he paces behind Leigh, a pair of rugby balls tucked under one arm, two more held in each hand, he walks with a rolling, agricultural gait, his close-cropped red hair receding from his forehead and temples to a pair of protruding ears. He is not especially big and his frame is softer-edged than you might expect. But Leigh's grandfather's statement is still impossible to deny. Anyone who knows their rugby also knows that Jenks is every inch 'the main man'.

In his thirteen-year international career Jenks racked

up more points than any Welsh player in history, scoring a total of eleven tries, 130 conversions, 235 penalties and ten drop goals. When he retired, he was the only player in the world to have scored more than a thousand international points. As he punts balls back down the pitch to Leigh this morning each kick betrays why that was the case. Every ball, nine years after Jenks hung up his boots, still lands with precision at Leigh's feet.

Between them Jenks and Leigh, coach and player, mentor and pupil, bridge the gap between rugby's amateur past and its professional future. Both Jenks and Leigh debuted young, at nineteen. Both had relatives putting in the hours in the wings: Leigh his grandfather; Jenks his uncles Peter and Andrew, drilling him towards a style and a rhythm on the training pitch at Pontypridd. But where Leigh came into the Wales set-up via the academies and a professional career, Jenks was filling a skip in his family's scrapyard when his father returned from the pub one day to tell him he was in the Welsh squad to face England. When he learnt about his second cap, he was tiling a council house and listening to the team announcement on a radio. Where Leigh built himself up through years of weights, strength programmes and supplements, Jenks was conditioned by swinging a sledgehammer or dragging an old tyre on shuttle runs in the alley behind his house. Jenks was a player formed in rugby's amateur era, driving lorries of scrap metal the length of Britain or working in Just Rentals between games. In contrast, Leigh has been shaped by the professional game, the hours of his days portioned by the training, media and fixture schedules of club and country.

Yet as they work together on the Castle pitch this morning, rehearsing the combinations that will unlock each kick, there is more shared territory between these two men than not. However much rugby has changed, there will always be fundamentals of a player's experience that will never alter and will continue to form strong bonds between the generations. For Leigh and Jenks the goal-kicker's ritual of solitary practice, that silent benediction exercised on a succession of empty pitches, has provided them with thousands of hours of shared experience. Though practised years apart, the two men's characters have been formed in the shadow of these repeated attempts to balance that ever-unstable equation of man, rugby ball and posts.

And then there have been those other shared experiences too. Rarer, but more intense, when under the stiletto-pressure of a match-day kick that coalface of practice is converted into a few diamond seconds under the eyes of millions. When a stadium and two stalled teams all wait upon the strike of your boot to tell them how, this time, the script will be written.

Over the years of their relationship the experience Leigh shares with Jenks has been deepened with inheritance. As with all the youngsters with whom he works, along with general skills advice Jenks has also passed on specifics of his own technique to Leigh. It's a lineage of knowledge that lies at the heart of Jenks's coaching philosophy, an ongoing attempt to undo one of the central paradoxes of rugby: that a player's knowledge will always progress in inverse proportion to the ability of their bodies. As a young player improves mentally, emotionally and technically, as he learns to read the game and himself better, so his body will slow and weaken with age and the violence of the sport.

Jenks reached the peak of his own playing knowledge towards the end of his career, when he had just a handful of games left. In coaching the lessons he's learnt to younger players now, Jenks hopes to shortcut them to that peak earlier in their own careers, and so increase the number of games in which their mental and technical skills are on a par with their physical ones. This is why he prefers to work with players like those kicking today – Rhys Priestland, James Hook and Leigh – from as early as fifteen or sixteen years old. Bad habits ruin more kickers than good habits make them. At eighteen or nineteen it's often too late; those bad habits are already stitched into a player's style. But at fifteen, sixteen Jenks knows he can build upon a player's skills without first having to unpick existing faults.

Although Jenks hasn't taken the field himself for almost a decade, his coaching work means a part of him still runs out with young players onto grounds across Wales every weekend. And a part of him still faces up to the posts on those grounds for the kicks at goal too. Every young kicker with whom he's worked eventually develops their own method, their own stance, approach and follow-through. But until they do they'll first glean what they can from the DNA of Jenks's kicking style. When the young Hunter S. Thompson decided to be a writer, he typed out the entire manuscript of F. Scott Fitzgerald's *The Great Gatsby*, just so he could 'feel' what writing a great novel might be like; its rhythms, pace and style. In a similar way young kickers working with Jenks will imitate the handwriting of his technique before creating their own, so they too can 'feel' how it might be to kick like one of the greatest in their game, before attempting to be so themselves.

The most important technique Jenks passed on to Leigh as a young player was psychological rather than physical. Wherever Jenks was kicking for goal, be it at the Arms Park in Cardiff, Kings Park in Durban or the Stade de France in Paris, as far as he was concerned he was never inside those stadia, but many miles away instead, on Cae Fardre, a field near his childhood home in Pentre'r Eglwys. With each of those kicks, as Jenks stepped back from the ball he also stepped back onto Cae Fardre, the place where he'd spent thousands of hours practising alone as a kid; where he'd kicked for fun and where things had always been easy.

Future visualisation is key in sport: the marksman sees the bullet penetrate the bull's eye before he shoots; the sprinter sees himself breast the line before he starts; and the goal-kicker sees the ball sailing through the posts before he makes the kick. But when Jenks was taking place kicks for Wales or the British Lions, his visualisation always projected two ways: forwards and backwards. Forwards to the successful kick, and backwards to those hours kicking alone on Cae Fardre. For Jenks, each place kick was also a kick about place: about using one location to protect himself from another, about drawing upon his memories of Cae Fardre so as to isolate himself from the pressures of the place in which he stood at that moment, facing up to the posts inside the crucible of a stadium.

It's this other dimension to 'place' kicking that Jenks has passed on to Leigh, so that now, when Leigh lines up a kick for Wales, it's another corner of the country that's conjured into stadia around the world: the pitch in Gorseinon where he and his grandfather first went to practise, and where they still go together whenever they can. Just as Cae Fardre used to insulate Jenks at the moment of a kick, so an image of Gorseinon, its trees and houses spreading through the Aviva Stadium in Dublin, insulated Leigh in Dublin that day from the gathering noise and whistles of the crowd as he quickened his steps towards the ball and, with just fifteen seconds left on the clock, struck it with all the power he could muster.

*Keep upright.*
>> *Make good contact.*
>>> *Follow through.*

The ball was still in the air when Leigh turned his back on that kick, and he was already running back to his teammates when the linesmen raised their flags. He knew the kick had been successful, and he knew that Wales had won. After the match, when he'd finished his interviews and his signings for fans and sponsors, Leigh found his grandfather and gave him the pair of boots with which he'd just kicked Wales to victory. The Irish match had begun with a try for one grandfather, and it was finished with a kick for another. In more ways than one Wales's first fixture in the Six Nations had been a game about starting points, foundations. *In my beginning,* as Eliot says, *is my end.*

Having taken just eight kicks at goal this morning Leigh and Jenks collect the balls and begin to make their way back to the team room up at the Vale. Eight kicks are all Leigh needs. These pre-match hours, for all the players, are a negotiation between preparation and freshness. About sharpening the blade without blunting it through overuse; about keeping as much in reserve as possible for the eighty minutes of the match ahead.

As they walk up towards the seventeenth-century turrets of Hensol Castle, which gives the training pitch its name, Leigh confides to Jenks that he's feeling more nervous than usual today, and for some reason he can't seem to shake it off.

'Enjoy it, butt,' Jenks tells him, giving him a pat on the shoulder. 'Give it your all.'

'All' is what rugby is to Jenks, and his all is what he's given the game. Which is why he knows about nerves. Within the squad he's as well known for his pre-match anxiety as he is for his kicking. Whether it's a fixture against Tenby or the All Blacks, whether playing or coaching, the run-up to every match will often see Jenks, wracked with nerves, retching in the changing rooms.

Jenks is also known within Welsh rugby for his encyclopedic knowledge of the game; for being able to tell you not only which team won on a certain date, but by how much and who scored when. If current players are still inheriting their aspirations from Jenks, then he in turn was first inspired by the players of the 1970s. When he was seven years old, he saw one of those Cardiff games in which Gerald Davies touched the ball four times and scored four tries. Ever since, fuelled by his rugby-playing uncles, he's been obsessed by the sport, *feeling* it even more than he knows it. During a match he lives every kick, break and tackle made by the players he coaches. Afterwards he'll absorb himself in analysing the patterns and plays. At the meal after the Irish match, as the two squads and their guests mingled around the tables talking and drinking, Jenks stood alone in a corner of the room, one hand in the pocket of his suit, the other holding a pint, looking up at a TV screen playing the match in which he'd just participated. It was as if even then, with the resonance of the game still fresh in the air and the grazes on the faces of the players still raw, Jenks wanted to see it all again, wanted to live it all again. As if, after all those months of preparation and training, he was reluctant to let those eighty minutes go.

For all the Wales coaches today the last forty-eight hours have been a slow process of letting go. Jenks, who will run messages during the match and be with the kickers for conversions and penalties, will have more contact with the players than most. But even for him, from the

Thursday of a match week onwards the majority of his work is done. Like a director and stage crew in the run-up to an opening night, Warren Gatland and his coaching team have to make the uncomfortable transition from being at the centre of the cast, the team, to becoming a member of the audience, the crowd.

This transition from influence to observation is one of the hardest parts of the coaches' jobs. As ex-players all of them first got involved in rugby to be on the field, and now they are off it, shaping policy and style of play, but unable to do anything at the moment of execution. As coaches they are still at the heart of the sport, so the sense of aftermath experienced by every ex-player is kept further at bay than for most. But on a match day that process is reversed, the proximity to the players and the game, the sound of the studs in the tunnel, the smells of strapping, mud and lubricant all magnifying rather than diminishing the distance between playing and not playing.

Even now, as Jenks enters the team room back at the Vale, although many of the coaching staff are in here with the players, sitting at the dining tables, looking through analyses on laptops, the impending match is already, minute by minute, opening the distances between them. Already they are growing apart. And yet the coaching relationship never ends, which is why all of the coaches, despite their own nerves or stress, will do their best to maintain an atmosphere of calm steadiness. In their own playing days teams and coaches often got psyched up, players shouting and head-butting walls in the changing rooms. But not today. Nowadays game day is about staying calm, about holding a level-headed gaze towards kick-off and what has to be done in the eighty minutes after it.

While in camp the team room is the heart of a rugby squad; a transplantable heart recreated in other hotels for away matches, and across the world when the squad goes on tour. At the Vale Resort the team room is on the lower ground level of the hotel, accessed through an innocuous-looking door in the lobby. Take a short flight of stairs down through a set of swing doors and you'll find yourself in a large, low-ceilinged room reminiscent of the lounge on a cross-channel ferry. In this room the fundamental elements of modern rugby are all within touching distance, lending it an atmosphere located somewhere between a canteen, a safe house, a student common room, a hospital ward and an Internet cafe.

Away from the Barn or the Castle training pitch, the team room is where the squad can be a team, and also themselves. Two floors above, where the press conferences are held, coaches and players adopt public personas. Their body language and rhythms of speech alter, slipping into the cyclical statements of the sports interview designed to inform but give nothing away. But as they descend the stairs from those press conferences the players shrug their characters back on like comfortable hoodies, allowing their limbs a greater freedom of expression and, in the case of the younger members of the squad, letting the years slip from their faces to reveal, once more, the boys within the men.

The first element of the team room you encounter on entering is the food, arranged on narrow tables along the left wall; a continually replenished row of silver-domed serving plates rotating through breakfast, lunch, snacks and dinner. Every day in pre-season each player will consume around 4,300 calories to keep their bodies going, with high intakes of protein for muscle growth, and essential and saturated fats for maximal anabolic effect. In season the calories will drop to around 4,070 a day, but the intake of carbohydrates will increase in proportion to the longer distances covered during matches and training, with squad menus continually reviewed by the WRU nutritionist Jon Williams. The majority of those calories will come from these tables in the team room, and for that reason 'players eat first' is the most sacred rule in here. This food is fuel, and it's the engine of the team that needs it the most.

At meal times the squad eats perfunctorily at a collection of round tables spread and laid in a wedding-like formation. Hunkering over their plates, their bodies seeming too big for the chairs, conversation is often minimal. An arrangement of supplements sits at the centre of each table, as if a chemist has taken charge of the decorations. Printed sheets beside these pill bottles remind the players of their 'SIX NATIONS 2012 SUPPLEMENT PROTOCOL':

## Daily Supplements

Maintain Beta Alanine, Aspartic Acid and Defence Daily

### Beetroot and Cherry Juice blend

Game Week – 4 cups per day

Training Week – 2 cups per day

Colostrum will be added to recovery shakes on game weeks to support immune system, aid recovery and improve gut health.

L-Carnitine will be added to shakes daily to aid recovery and fat loss.

In the toilets plastic vials for tests by the in-house medics are scattered about the sinks.

Close by the dining tables, and facing the food on the far wall, is a row of other tables on which the squad also spend hours of their time each week. These are the physio and massage tables on which, as some of the squad eat a meal, others will be lying, stripped to their underwear to receive treatments from the physios. Occasionally a blue-gloved dentist performs dental work in this area too. Fuel and repair, fuel and repair: the team room is also a pit stop.

Pool and table-tennis tables at the centre of the room provide the main leisure activities, while beyond these a bank of WRU laptops are in constant use for video analysis, emailing, tweeting and downloading music and films. Behind a set of sofas another table is kept stocked with shirts, rugby balls and posters for the players to sign as they pass in and out of the room. Over the last two weeks this table's surface has been increasingly obscured under the piles of signature requests and merchandise. Taped to the wall opposite, beside a Powerade drinks fridge, are the latest judgements of the fines committee:

Jug – Wrong kit – £20
Foxy – Late to units – £10
Bomb – Late physio/no watch – £30

As well as being the heart of the Welsh camp, the team room is also its hive brain. This is where the hydra-headed animal that is a team communicates with itself, where its tone and consciousness is set and can be measured. Step into this room on a Monday after a match and the atmosphere within these walls will immediately tell you whether the game was won or lost. This is where Thumper's weddings and funerals are lived, the wake of each match turning the air light and charged or dense and oppressive, depending on the result.

Movement within the team room, as elsewhere in the camp, is governed by the day sheet: the daily schedule of training, treatments, meetings and media duties handed out by Thumper the night before. Without announcement or instruction players and staff will drift like a shoal towards the seats in front of the projection screen and a defence or attack meeting will begin, as if triggered purely by the weight of bodies in that part of the room. Together with the day sheet's instructions on which kit should be worn, such an apparently unconducted movement by so many men wearing identical clothes further heightens the sense of a herd mentality within camp; the blending of tens of individuals, many of whom regularly compete against each other for their clubs, into a single organism.

In one corner of the team room a pair of electronic scales are wired up to a couple of laptops on shoulder-height stands. On first entering the room every morning the players gravitate towards these machines before eating their breakfast. Standing on the scales they answer a series of programmed questions, tapping in their responses on the touch screens of the laptops.

*On a scale of one to five, how did they sleep?*
*What is their mood?*
*Any hint of a cold?*

An outline of a body appears on the screen.

*Do they have any aches and pains?*

If they do (and they nearly always do), the players press the on-screen body in the places where their own is hurting. By the end of breakfast their answers to these questions will already have been processed and sent directly to the iPhones and computers of the head of physical performance, head of medical and Warren Gatland.

Before the players reach the computerised monitoring station they will more than likely already have said good morning to Dan Baugh, the assistant strength and conditioning coach. Those who haven't are sure to see the barrel-chested Canadian approaching them soon afterwards, his hand outstretched in greeting. With a shaved head, beard and Heston Blumenthal glasses, Dan resembles a Hell's Angel bouncer moonlighting as a lab technician. But when he says 'Good morning' to a player, there's nothing intimidating about his voice, just a genuine warmth running through an accent falling somewhere between a Seattle rock singer and an Alberta lumberjack.

This is how Dan prefers to monitor players, rather than rely solely on the £30,000-worth of computer equipment in the corner of the team room. 'I'd rather shake hands, always have,' he says. 'I got it from the French clubs. First greeting of the day there, it's tradition to shake hands, look someone in the eye, ask 'em how they're feeling.'

This personal contact is vital to Dan and is at the heart of his approach to coaching. He has an MA in Coaching Science, including a dissertation on 'Emerging Defensive Philosophies in World Rugby', so he more than understands the changing landscape of the modern game, the need to keep at the cutting edge. But in an environment where levels of technology and scrutiny mean there are increasingly few places for a player to hide his moods and emotions, Dan also tries to make the Welsh camp as personal as possible.

'People ask me what we do up here, what's so special about it? And I say we hug a lot. I tell the guys I love 'em all the time. Every aspect of the international game is pretty shitty. It's intense, physically and mentally, you put your body under ridiculous stress. But family fights harder than friends, y'know? You have to really care about the people you work with. On a subconscious level the body can react slower if you don't care for your teammate.'

As a flanker for Cardiff in the late 1990s and early 2000s Dan knows there was a time when international players relished returning to their clubs from the Welsh camp. This was often because they were returning from an impersonal environment into more of a family set-up. Now he hopes the Welsh coaching team have reversed that process. 'I know the guys can't wait to get back into camp, get back together. And that's great, because the closer we become, the better we become.'

But Dan's morning handshakes and hugs are as much for him as they are for the players. Compared to the monitoring computers, he personally finds the French method a more comprehensive barometer of a player's well-being, especially as the squad near game day.

'People are much more comfortable saying to you socially that they didn't sleep well, and I mean, there's nowhere on that monitoring thing to say your wife told you to fuck off or that something bad has happened. All the touchy-feely stuff that doesn't go on the computers you can talk about, clear the air. Then, when selection comes into this, all of a sudden on the monitoring kit everyone feels great, all of a sudden everyone slept well, all of a sudden the ratings say, "I'm ready, pick me!" So I shake their hands instead, get some eye contact.'

It was a more robust kind of contact that first brought Dan into rugby at the age of sixteen. He was involved in judo and wrestling since he was four, so physical, combative sport had always been a defining principle in his life. One day, though, in a period when he was playing a lot of Canadian football, some friends asked if he'd join them at rugby training. After just one session Dan knew he'd discovered his calling. As rugby took over, his other sports soon began falling away.

'I just loved the fact there were no pads, that I could hit people, and at the time there were no red or yellow cards so I could get into fights. It was a man's game, y'know? I was a kid, but I was being treated like a man.'

Within a year of picking up a rugby ball Dan represented Canada at under-16s. He went on to represent his country at every age group, playing against Wales at Fletcher's Fields in 1997. His physical style of play caught the eye of some of the Cardiff players in the side, so when, a year later, the Welsh captain and Cardiff flanker Gwyn Jones broke his neck, it was Dan who Cardiff called. As is so often the case in rugby, an opportunity came his way through another man's injury and at the cost of another player's career.

Under the alias of Dan Brown, Dan was asked to trial for Gwyn's place in the Blues. He made the trip across the Atlantic and, after impressing his new bosses on the pitch, never went back, going on to play for Cardiff for another seven years. He soon became a popular player with the Cardiff fans, infamous for the physicality of his tackles and his running game, until eventually his style of play took its toll and a broken foot retired him into coaching. Gwyn's injury opened the door for Dan into European rugby and, at just thirty, another injury closed it again.

But only as a player. Six years later, having joined the Welsh set-up full-time in the summer, Dan has spent this morning at the Vale following his usual strict match-day routine. For once he didn't greet the players over breakfast, and he didn't look them in the eye and ask them how they're feeling. He knows he can be intense on game day, and that the last thing a player needs is 'some super-psyched-up guy sitting in the corner with big eyes'. So he's kept his distance and is focusing on his match-day roles instead: running the primers and preparing for his pre-match warm-up with the team and the subs in the stadium.

Dan has brought many principles from his Canadian sporting days into his work with the Wales squad. In the 'Red Room', a padded area at the end of the gym, he regularly works on the close-quarters strength players need in rucks and mauls, drawing upon his experience in judo, wrestling and grappling. His training technique of functional blocks owes more than a nod to his past in Canadian football, while the 'play-off' facial hair he grows for every tournament is a tradition inherited from Canadian ice hockey.

For this Six Nations Dan chose an Amish-style beard with no moustache or sideburns, which now, on the morning of Wales's final game, after six weeks of competition, has grown as far as the collar of his tracksuit. He has no idea how the dice will fall today. He's seen how hard the squad have worked, and knows how hard he and Adam Beard pushed them once again in Poland. He also knows this is a squad who are close, who will fight for each other as much as for themselves. But the French have come to Cardiff to win, and have a history of spoiling the party for the best teams in the world. So, as ever, there is no certainty, no foreknowledge, other than that this evening, whichever way the scoreline falls, Dan will be able to shave.

Dan and Adam work closely together and share a similar vision. And yet in many ways the two men are the direct opposite of each other. Where Dan has a trucker's bulk, Adam has the compact physique of a gymnast.

Where Dan is loud and in your face, Adam is quieter and more attuned to subtler forms of persuasion. Where Adam is thorough, Dan's preparations can verge on OCD. Where Dan, in his own words, is 'very hands-on, a bit of a grunt, a grunt with a voice', Adam is an academic. The relationship is not without its tensions – again, by Dan's own admission he's 'a number two who sees himself as a number one' – but without doubt it's a combination that works.

This pattern of complementary opposition is repeated across the Wales management. In contrast to the increased physical and temperamental uniformity of the modern player, the diversity of the Welsh coaching staff, in appearance and personality, still reflects how multifaceted a sport rugby is, and is a reminder of the huge range of qualities the game demands of its players. Within each area of the Wales set-up, men work cheek-by-jowl with colleagues who, like Adam and Dan, often appear to be polar opposites. But however mismatched the components may appear, the mechanism as a whole works smoothly again and again, not in spite, but *because* of these differences.

At the physio tables in the team room Prav Mathema, the head of medical performance, works alongside Mark Davies, or 'Carcass', as he's known within the squad. In contrast to Prav's easy-going energy and default smile, Carcass, an ex-international himself, is the squad's stoic, possessed of a granite-like stillness and a 'wise man of the mountain' air. Where Carcass is sparse of speech, Prav is talkative; where Carcass is tall, Prav is shorter. If Prav's approachable manner and gelled hair are those of an affable TV presenter, then Carcass, with his thousand-yard touchline stare and motionless, broken-nosed profile, is more reminiscent of an Easter Island statue that's done time in the ring.

The differing personalities of the coaches who work alongside Jenks on the squad's defence, attack and forward play are all rooted in their respective roles, with each man embodying the traits of his specialism. Rob Howley, the Wales attack coach and one of the country's greatest-ever scrum-halves, is quick and involved, as alert to nuance and lateral vision in his coaching off the field as he was in his playing days on it. As he moves between the players on the training pitch or harries them through patterns of attack in the Barn, Rob's natural expression is one of furrowed concern, betraying a restless mind always on the lookout for the unexplored strategy, the gap to exploit.

As a player Rob had to punch above his weight from an early age, having been told on more than one occasion that he was too small or too slight to make it in international rugby. But the schoolboy who'd spent his weekends playing out his dreams of captaining Wales on the local park behind Priory Avenue in Bridgend was not going to be denied. Having made the Wales number-nine jersey his, he finally ran out to captain Wales against Italy in 1997. The circumstances, however, were not as Rob would have wished. His opportunity came, like Dan's, in the wake of the previous captain, Gwyn Jones, breaking his neck. Unlike Dan, Rob knew Gwyn well and had spent much of the weeks before that Italy game beside his hospital bed as his friend came to terms with being told that he may never walk again.

Gwyn supported Rob's appointment as captain, and Rob went on to lead Wales to their greatest number of successive victories ever. He was also, though, captain through some of the country's most difficult periods, and it's this mixed experience of success and failure that appears to drive Rob: the tenacity of the underdog coupled with the drive of a winner; the scent of success married with a heightened awareness of its fragility.

On first meeting Shaun Edwards, the Wales defence coach, he can seem as impregnable as the strategies he's woven into the fabric of the squad, his set pit-bull expression imprinted with the same ethos as his rugby – *Thou shalt not pass*. But those who get to know Shaun get to know the depths of the man, and with them, closer to his core, a certain warmth. Possessed of a strong sense of 'code', of what is and isn't important in life, gained from his time as a rugby-league player for Wigan and Great Britain, Shaun is possibly the most decorated player in the country, his broken nose and the scars on his bald head testament to the extent to which he's lived his learning. That he would live a life immersed in rugby was never in question. His father played professionally for Wigan, until, at the age of twenty-four, a spinal injury almost crippled him. Unable to play himself, Shaun says his father didn't so much push him into the game 'as kick me in'. As a young boy he'd sleep with a rugby ball in his bed, and every day he walked past Wigan's ground at Central Park on his way to and from school. At the age of just seventeen, that ground became his new destination when the club signed the schoolboy Shaun for a record-breaking £35,000.

Had it not been for his strong desire to live near James, the son he had with Heather Small, the lead singer of M People, Wigan might still have Shaun now. As it was, Shaun chose to move south to be closer to James. Having switched codes he became head coach at Wasps in West London, before Warren Gatland brought him across the border to shore up the Welsh defence.

Suitably, perhaps, for a devout Catholic who counts priests and monks among his closest friends and family, there is more than a touch of the Shaolin monk about Shaun's position within the Wales set-up. Fiercely individual, seemingly immune to the day sheet's kit instructions, Shaun is a reader and a thinker, existing along a tensile fault line between the intellectual and the physical. When analysing a game, he does so with the vision of a chess player, explaining the multiple patterns and attacking possibilities in a soft Manchester accent frequently lifted and quickened by an enthusiast's passion.

Praise from Shaun is a rare jewel, and as such is valued all the more highly among the players.

As the Wales forwards coach, Rob McBryde is responsible for the set pieces of the game, the line-outs and scrums upon which Shaun's defensive strategies and Rob Howley's patterns of attack are built. And Rob is, indeed, as 'set' a character as the tightly packed scrummaging formations he oversees. Solid, thick-necked and boulder-shouldered, there's something of the carthorse's reliable strength about Rob. Capped for Wales at hooker and selected for the British Lions tour to Australia in 2001, he was also once crowned 'Wales's Strongest Man'. Of North Walian stock, his laconic presence at training is reminiscent of a hill farmer come into town for a cattle auction. But there's something timeless about Rob too, his mountain-worn manner sounding a strong note against R. S. Thomas's closing lines on Iago Prytherch;

> Remember him, then, for he, too, is a winner of
> wars,
> Enduring like a tree under the curious stars.

As a first-language Welsh speaker, Rob moves easily between the Welsh and English spoken by the players in the squad. In 2007 he took on the bardic duty of Grand Sword Bearer at the National Eisteddfod, accepting the mantle from its former title-holder, the late Ray Gravell. It's a role that fits Rob well. Where others might look awkward or out of place in a druid's robes, when Rob holds that ceremonial sword aloft he looks all too authentic, and it's no stretch of the imagination to picture him wielding it in the defence of his country a thousand years ago.

Warren Gatland, or 'Gats', the man who manages and has this coaching team at his disposal, is the still point at its centre; a locking pin around which the daily work in camp revolves. With a plaintive set to his eyes and close-cropped silver hair, Warren moves slow and easy about the training pitch like a tracksuited, philosophical teddy bear, his hands in his pockets, assured yet approachable, open to the world yet lost in private thought.

Straight talking, sometimes to his own detriment, Warren also knows how to weigh the power of silence. Before a game he often won't speak in the changing rooms but will just stand at its centre, the players preparing around him, his head bowed, arms crossed, sometimes padding out a pattern of small repetitive steps, as if performing a meditative ritual.

It's a sparse verbal style suited to the nature of the squad, or perhaps the squad have suited themselves to Warren. Either way, much of the communication in the Welsh camp is non-verbal, a gesture or a look doing the work of sentences. Even at the rugby sessions on the Castle training pitch Warren and the other coaches are minimal in their vocal instruction. The players themselves will erupt into frantic calling and shouting when running moves or doing rucking and spidering sessions, sounding disturbingly like soldiers caught in sudden contact. But on the whole Warren will reserve his voice for afterwards, for when the squad gather round him at the centre of the pitch, hands resting on knees to catch their breaths, leaning in to listen. At the end of these training sessions, just as in the changing room, Warren will often just stand on the halfway line, arms folded, as with a syncopated pattern of hollow punts and thuds the squad practise their various kicks, the balls rising and falling about him like brief constellations.

At these moments Warren embodies the coach as observer, silently weighing the attributes of the players and staff around him. But his are far from the only eyes watching training. At every session there are always cameras too, mounted on poles, tripods or hand-held by one of the team of analysts. The man who oversees this team and the information they collect is Rhys Long, a big no-nonsense thirty-something with spiky dark hair who, as he puts it himself, 'is paid to watch rugby'.

Rhys was brought up in what is arguably the capital of British rugby analysis, Porthcawl, a small seaside town in South Wales. Just as neighbouring Port Talbot produces a disproportionate number of actors, so Porthcawl can lay claim to the head analysts of Wales, England, New Zealand, Exeter and Wasps, plus three more at the English Institute of Sport. As a young field, performance analysts make up a small community, and most of these men were at Rhys's wedding. His best friend, Michael Hughes, the lead analyst for England, was also his best man.

It's Michael's father, whom Rhys refers to as 'the god-father of analysis, the oracle', who is responsible for Porthcawl's association with performance analysis. As an early pioneer in the field he moved his family to the town when he took up a position at the University of Wales Institute, Cardiff. Michael was eleven at the time, an age when school friends were impressed by a father who made his living from studying the intricacies of sports.

Rhys, however, was going to be a professional rugby player, and had Adam Jones not fallen on his leg during an under-21s trial, breaking his tibia and ankle, then he may have still lived out his dream. He was playing at number eight for Bridgend at the time. The club had begun using an early version of Sportscode, software for sports analysis. As Rhys recovered from his injury, and knowing he was unlikely to return to playing, he 'began messing around with it to see what it could do'. That messing around led Rhys, four years later, to the Welsh camp, where, since 2007, he's upgraded and run their analysis.

His working methods are something of a 'push–pull' process. As he says, 'A good analyst stays close to their coaches.' So much of what he does is in response to what they want to achieve, to what they find effective and help-ful in pursuing the model or policy they already have in place. But at the same time Rhys will also initiate changes in training according to the nature of his findings. When his analysis revealed the Wales centre pairing had the lowest passing efficiency of all the Welsh regions, Rob Howley introduced a rigorous passing programme into their training schedule and their efficiency improved. Similarly, if certain players have a low record of success in the air or under high balls, training drills are developed to counter these weaknesses. 'None of it is revolutionary,' Rhys says. 'It's about aggregation of marginal gains. If you improve by 1 per cent in twenty different areas, then that's a 20 per cent improvement overall.'

During the Six Nations this process of response and initiation is further complicated by the tight schedule of fixtures. With a match nearly every week, Rhys constantly has to look both ways, analysing Wales's performance against the team just played and analysing the team they are about to play. It's a delicate balance. Over-responding to readings from last week's game against Ireland might be counterproductive if this week's opponents, Scotland, play a totally different style of rugby. 'It is', Rhys says, 'like trying to stay one step ahead, but one step behind too.'

Although most of Rhys's working time is spent analysing Wales's performance on the field, his analytical mind can't help drawing from information off it too. One of the strengths of this current squad, he thinks, is their grounding beyond rugby. Many of the players have strong families, older brothers, roots to which they return. A relatively high proportion have stable, settled home lives. Others, however, he admits, play better when not attached, as if 'they need that George Best swagger to play their best game'. According to Rhys, though, Wales's greatest strength is what some in the past have cited as their greatest weakness. 'It's our size,' he explains. 'Our ability to assemble the squad quickly, to centralise everything here. All the boys live close by so they can drop in any time, see Prav or Carcass if they're injured. While they're in camp, our boys, if they want to, go home on a Tuesday night, stay home Wednesday and come in again Thursday. They can see their families, wives, girlfriends, sleep in their own beds. It's like Wales', Rhys says proudly, 'is the biggest club team in the world.'

Every coach, on taking responsibility for a team, will try to create a culture: a foundation of principles and attitudes around which a squad can bond, and to which new members can aspire. Although Warren brought a hive of Wasps into the Wales set-up – Shaun, Rhys, Howley and Prav all having worked for the London club he used to coach – he was still, in many ways, a stranger entering a tightly knit family. In this situation most coaches will use a change of culture as a short-cut to evoking new ties and cohesion. Warren's greatest strength, however, is that rather than try and create such a culture, he *is* the culture.

The current Welsh squad's personality is an imprint

of Warren's own: honest, hard-working, level-headed and accepting of its own responsibility. It's a coaching style Warren partly inherited from those who coached him through school, club and national levels back in New Zealand: men such as Glenn Ross, Kevin Greene and Alex Wyllie. But his coaching philosophy also owes something to his time working as a teacher in the country too. Rugby players are, he says, 'often like big kids', so applying the principles of teaching makes sense to Warren. Meetings are kept short, points to remember kept to as few as possible, and loyalty won through honesty and fair treatment. The resulting coaching style is perhaps more subtle and roundabout than most, reliant upon empowering an individual rather than loading them with information, but the end 'product', Warren feels, is worth it.

'How many test caps you got now?' he'll casually ask one of his young backs, drawing the question through a languid Kiwi accent. When they tell him twenty-nine or thirty, Warren will raise his eyebrows. 'Yeah?' he'll say, a surprised pitch rising through the word. 'That's a lot. You must be one of the most experienced out there, eh? You should be talking a lot. You talking a lot out there?' And the seed, Warren hopes, is sown. Despite being only twenty-two or twenty-three, the player walks away having been given the nod, and the nudge, that as a relative elder statesman they have the licence to play like one.

That coaching can be about giving time as well as

taking it is an aspect of the role Warren understands. Family, he says, comes first. If a player needs a day off because their wife is having a scan, or because there's trouble in the marriage, then Warren would rather lose that player for a day or a week, and win their loyalty in doing so, than keep them in camp and lose it further down the line. Having coached in the northern hemisphere for over twenty years, but with his wife Trudy and son Bryn still living in New Zealand, Warren is no stranger to the strains rugby can put on family life. It is, as he often says when talking about rugby, an ongoing question of balance and negotiation. About knowing when to put the pressure on, and when to ease off.

Today, with still four hours until the anthems, it's time to ease off; a time for restraint, for not over-coaching so close to a match. Because of this, Warren will keep to himself for much of the day and will try his best not to broadcast his nerves to the squad. The first time he'll see them will be for the walk-through of moves and line-outs. Then, like all the coaches, it'll be about keeping to his match-day routine until the team meeting and the boarding of the bus. Rob Howley will use this time to call home and speak to his wife and kids, absorbing himself in their plans for the day rather than his own, which are already being broadcast across the country. Rob McBryde will go to the gym, get a feel for the mood of the players over breakfast, then 'stick his head in a book' to pass the time. Shaun, too, will try and say as little as possible to the players, and will also often read a book. When he was a player, together with praying before a match, reading was a technique Shaun often used to cope with his nerves. It's one he passes on to some of the players too. Sometimes he will even take his book up into the coaching box, and he has been known to carry on reading it while in there.

Whatever their routine or habits, all the coaches will try and use this period of the day to focus on their roles and do whatever they can to kill time, until the only time that matters finally arrives: the eighty minutes of Wales against France, played in the Millennium Stadium by a squad they've relentlessly coached, advised and analysed, and whose fortunes and well-being have consumed the last ten weeks of their lives.

On taking charge of Wales in 2007, Warren switched the home changing room in the Millennium Stadium from the northern side of the players' tunnel to the southern. The years preceding his tenure had been unstable and volatile. The spark of brilliance that won Wales a Grand Slam in 2005 was soon extinguished by rifts between players and coaches. A series of stuttering performances finally culminated in a pool-stage knockout by Fiji in the 2007 World Cup. Warren wanted a new start for the Welsh team, a new home within their home. So he moved their dressing room down the corridor, meaning that instead of turning right off their bus Wales now turn left to enter the four dragon-painted rooms that make up their changing rooms within the stadium.

Those four linked rooms are where J.R., the squad's kit man, has been working for most of the morning, preparing them for the arrival of the team. Having arrived himself at 9.30 a.m., he's spent the last hour and a half, as he has for every Welsh game since 1985, unloading equipment from his van, laying out the players' kit and clipping in their names and cap numbers above their changing stalls.

Sometimes J.R. works in silence. When he does, there is something of the Catholic ritual about his process, a solitary and sombre dedication at twenty-two separate altars. This morning, however, he's been working to music playing from an iPod dock plugged into the side of Adam Jones's stall. 'Living on a Prayer', 'More Than a Woman' and the Stereophonics' 'Local Boy in the Photograph' have all animated the low-ceilinged space as J.R., occasionally slipping his glasses to the end of his nose to read the label of a shirt, prepares the room. Moving around the three-sided changing area in an anticlockwise direction, he builds the folded piles of kit on the right-hand side of each player's bench, working in reverse order to what they'll need first. He begins with the white towels, folding each one as meticulously as a Savoy chambermaid, before dropping them to the benches with a series of soft rhythmical thuds. The dark wood of the changing stalls makes them appear all the brighter, a comforting reward or consolation waiting for each player after their eighty minutes of violent exertion.

Upon each towel J.R. lays a pair of red and white socks, a pair of white shorts, a red training top and a red Welsh shirt, its number facing up. Taking each item of clothing fresh from its packaging he inspects it, then folds it with precision. As he lays down each player's shirt, he gives it a single stroke across the number on its back, as if calming a highly strung animal or bestowing a brief blessing upon its wearer. The numbers themselves are composed of thousands of images of fans' faces. Together with the word '*Braint*' inside the collar, these faces are a further reminder for whom the squad are playing when they put on these shirts, and never more so than today, when the weight of Welsh fans' expectations will press heavier upon their backs than ever.

J.R.'s manner and appearance as he works in the Wales changing rooms is reminiscent of an owner of a hardware store, the kind of blue-aproned shopkeeper who'll shake his head as he studies your list, before retrieving even the most unlikely of parts from his cupboards. Although J.R. says he sees himself at the bottom of the ladder within the Welsh squad, he'll be quick to point out, in his matter-of-fact Barry Island accent, that 'you can't play a game without kit, without the kit man you can't play the game', the mirroring of his syntax lending a further inevitability to his role.

He's right, but there's another reason for the fundamental quality of J.R.'s presence too. Having first worked for the Welsh team in 1985, J.R., as he'll tell you himself, 'has more bloody caps than anyone'. Over the last twenty-seven years, as he's gone about his duties, J.R., like Lee and Craig in the groundsman's office, has seen hundreds of players and coaches pass through the team. He was already established within the squad when the current home-grown Wales coaches all got their first caps, when the WRU chairman, Dai Pickering, was captaining the side and when a young Rob Howley 'wanted a cup of tea and a chat'. In an environment of flux, in which players, kit and coaches change all the time, J.R. is a rare seam of continuity within the Wales set-up, his knowing world-weariness, as if nothing could surprise him, lending him the air of a minor Shakespearean character moving among the brief tragedies and triumphs of the players and coaches. Like the porter in *Macbeth* who, as Macbeth wracks himself with worries about his destiny, goes about his business, having seen many great men come and go through his gates, so J.R. keeps his vision close, occupying himself with the necessities of his role and little more.

As J.R. works in the Welsh changing rooms, singing along to M. C. Hammer's 'Hammer Time', he is surrounded by the symbolism of his country. The WRU's version of the Prince of Wales feathers is imprinted at the back of each player's stall, and again across the entrance to the changing area. In the gym next door a bright-red dragon, its claw raised, fills the floor space between the weights machines. Dragons appear again on the Welsh flags hung throughout the other rooms, and a dragon's tail coils between the statements written above the players' heads: 'RESPECT THE JERSEY', '*DAL DY DIR*'.

Other text around the room is more specific, telling the story of the match to come later today. A list of players to be strapped by the physio teams is written in black marker pen on white medical tape stuck to the wall:

**Team I**
George
Smiler

**Team II**
Jug
Luke

Tips                                        Alun
Bom
Cuth
Yanto


On a whiteboard above a table of Powerade drinks
the pre-match schedule for the Italy game is still written
up in blue, its timings yet to be replaced with those for
today:

14.02 – Come together – melon
14.03 – Leave changing rooms
14.04 – Warm up with Beardy
14.09 – Squad together – short and long passing
14.11 – Split
14.15 – Defence
14.19 – Back to changing rooms
14.26 – Wales out
14.27 – Anthems
14.29 – Bag hits
14.30 – Kick-off


Elsewhere, on several walls throughout the four rooms,
those banners appear again:

*Yesterday is in the past.*
*How do you want to be remembered?*

When Wales played England this year, it was J.R.'s responsibility to recreate this home changing room within the aircraft carrier that is the stadium at Twickenham. Denuded of stalls or any of the symbols painted on these walls, J.R. brought the squad's equipment from Cardiff, hung Welsh flags above the players' benches and put up two new banners. The first, hanging in the physio area, read:

WINNERS DON'T WAIT
FOR CHANCES THEY
**TAKE THEM**.

The second, hung above the whiteboard written up with the pre-match schedule, where everyone could see it, told the players:

BE PREPARED TO **SUFFER**.

If proof were ever needed that when two national rugby teams come together on a pitch, it's never just two sides that meet, but two cultures, two histories, then for over a century the annual Wales vs England fixture has been all the evidence required. Historically attuned as sport is, few other matches are so invested with meaning. Every year the eighty minutes of these games have been fuelled by centuries of association, either drawing upon the perennial Welsh grievance of oppression by a 'recently arrived' more powerful neighbour, or stoked by contemporary events such as the flooding of Welsh valleys for English reservoirs or Margaret Thatcher's heavy hand in the miners' strike. Culturally, each game against England is, too, a reminder of the class difference at the root of the sport in each nation. As J.R. was recreating the Welsh changing room in Twickenham that day, English supporters were already arriving in the car park outside to unpack hampers of champagne and caviar from their Range Rovers.

In his pre-match speech in 1977, the Welsh captain, Phil Bennett, openly drew upon the fractious relationship between the two nations:

Look what these bastards have done to Wales. They've taken our coal, our water, our steel. They buy our homes and live in them for a fortnight every year. What have they given us? Absolutely nothing. We've been exploited, raped, controlled and punished by the English – and that's who you are playing this afternoon.

When the teams met ten years later in Cardiff, the crowd witnessed what has since been described as the most violent twenty minutes of Six Nations rugby ever, with four players eventually banned after the match.

But that was then. Now, along with professionalism,

things have changed. The contemporary Welsh players, some of whom were born in England or who have an English parent, have moved beyond an emotional response to the English game towards a more focused perspective. As Warren has warned them, 'Emotional energy can catch a team out.' The fixture is still undeniably charged, but where many Wales supporters would say that beating England is still more important than winning the other matches in the rest of the Six Nations, the players, if they are to bring about that win, have to see things differently.

England presented a significant challenge for Wales this year. An equally young side, they were ambitious to salvage their reputation after a disastrous World Cup and eager to perform well for their caretaker coach, Stuart Lancaster. They were also, like Wales, currently unbeaten in the tournament, having scraped through two wins against Italy and Scotland. Whoever won at Twickenham stood a good chance of winning the Grand Slam. And so it was that Sam Warburton and his team prepared themselves for a physically intense match, not in the way of punches thrown in animosity, but in the way of a fast, hard game motivated purely by the desire to win.

Although Wales were favourites going into the match, the statistics were stacked against them. In twenty-four years they'd only ever beaten England at Twickenham twice, and never before had they won a Triple Crown, the trophy in their sights that day, on English soil. Changes to the side included the young Ken Owens starting at hooker, replacing the more experienced veterans Huw Bennett and Matthew Rees. Dealing with the positive expectation, meanwhile, rather than their more familiar role of underdogs at Twickenham, would be a test of the squad's character as a whole.

The nature of that expectation, after their first two victories over Ireland and Scotland, was apparent in Wales's arrival at the stadium, both in the tone of their reception and the tone of their entrance. When the English team had arrived, looking crisply sharp with gelled hair and wafts of aftershave, although the fans outside welcomed them with baying support there was barely a tremor of response within the stadium. When Wales entered a few minutes later, having walked through the taunts of those same fans, the cleaners stopped cleaning, a handful of Royal Marines came in from the pitch and the RFU backroom staff stalled in their pre-match tasks, all to catch a glimpse of the Welsh squad arriving. As Wales came into the corridor between the changing rooms, they did so with an air of dark intent. Moving in single file, eyes forward, not a single man acknowledged those watching them. Their massed bulk, witnessed in succession, was as weighted with unremitting opposition as the opening bars of Mahler's Fifth.

Wales were here to make history, that's what their entrance seemed to say. Inside the changing room itself, Shaun Edwards and Rhys Long had spelt out exactly how they intended to achieve that in five points on the game's tip sheet, left on the players' benches under each of their folded towels:

1. Don't hurt ourselves – charge downs, intercepts, sin bins.
2. Smash their L/O drives – our width is vital after a breakout.
3. Muscle up on T—, M—, F— and C—
   EXTRA AGGRESSION ON **R—**
   **– SMOKE TARGET**
4. Speed into position. Work hard early.
5. Keep square off the line.

Following these points, in case there was any doubt, were two further statements, brutal in their simplicity, and a concession target for which to aim:

ASSAULT THEIR ATTACK.
BE RELENTLESS.
12/13 POINTS TARGET.

The English match was every bit as physical as Wales expected. Sam went to the post-match dinner with stitches in his eye, while Leigh Halfpenny had to endure the hits that came with England kicking to the corners throughout the whole eighty minutes. It was also, however, much tighter than they expected: down-to-the-wire close, with the final score of England 12 – Wales 19 exactly hitting Shaun's projected concession of points.

But it could have been so much worse. When Rhys Priestland was sin-binned for an offside tackle at the start of the second half, Wales, once again, had to play for ten minutes with just fourteen men. The last time they'd been a man down at Twickenham they'd conceded seventeen points. This time, however, with Mike Phillips bossing the game with a series of pick and drives, they held onto possession for eight and a half minutes and not only conceded no points, but also scored three through a penalty by Leigh. When Rhys took the field again, the score stood at England 12 – Wales 9, and a significant psychological contest had been won. But the match itself still wasn't, and wouldn't be until the seventy-sixth minute, when a moment of individual brilliance from a player off the bench finally snatched victory for Wales.

There's something of a tradition in Wales of such moments providing the turning point in matches against England: Ieuan Evans out-sprinting Rory Underwood in 1993 to secure a 10–9 victory; Scott Gibbs's last-minute crash and jink under the posts to set up Jenks's conversion that put England away 32–31 at Wembley in 1999; Gavin Henson's seventy-sixth-minute long-range penalty to beat them again in 2005.

In 2012 it would be another Scott who helped Wales turn the corner: Scott Williams, a twenty-one-year-old centre who just a year earlier had been training as a plumber. With only five minutes left on the clock, Scott, having come on for the injured Jamie Roberts, followed the advice of that banner in the changing room and, when he saw it, took his opportunity. As Courtney Lawes, the English second row, was being tackled by Sam on the halfway line, Scott ripped the ball from his arms and grubber-kicked it past the English defence. Judging the bounce as he accelerated in pursuit, he gathered the ball as it rose sweetly to his right and away from Tom Croft, the English flanker bearing down on his left.

'If it had gone the other way,' Scott later acknowledged in his laidback Carmarthenshire accent, 'then I reckon he'd have got me.' But it didn't, and Croft didn't, so with an arm raised in celebration Scott dived across the English line, untouched by opposition hands. For the first time in the match Wales were ahead and, following Leigh's conversion, seven points in the lead. Five minutes later, after David Strettle's last-ditch lunge across the Welsh line was ruled 'inconclusive', the match was over and Wales had won. Within a further fifteen minutes the careful order of J.R.'s changing room was undone by the disorder of victory, with pizza boxes, beer bottles and muddied kit strewn across the floor. The suited management stood in the middle of the half-dressed players, beaming as Gethin Jenkins put on a celebratory playlist and the Triple Crown, like the treasured loot it was, was passed from hand to hand for posed photos on iPhones and cameras.

In the midst of their celebrations, however, many of the Welsh players were also anxious to leave the changing room. Since using cryotherapy in Spała and Gdansk, the squad had employed the services of a mobile cryolab to enable them to continue the treatment throughout the Six Nations. In the weeks between each match this van, converted from a police command unit and run by an evangelical former rugby player called Karl, has parked up in the country lane at the back of the Barn. As the local farmer herds his cattle between the lane's hedges, down the road Welsh players have queued up twice a day to enter its futuristic silver pod for three minutes of extreme freezing. At home matches Karl parks the van in the subterranean passageways of the Millennium Stadium, but at Twickenham the RFU restricted him to the public car park. So this is where the Welsh players headed after the game, barefoot and chaperoned by Adam Beard, his head often reaching no higher than their shoulders. The crowd of thousands was still streaming out of the stadium, but this didn't deter Sam and his team, or blur their focus in getting to the cryolab for their three minutes of treatment. Cryotherapy, by this stage of the tournament, had become something else for the squad: a crucial psychological as well as physical tool, as much a ritual of belief as a method of recovery.

As one by one the Welsh players left the raucous celebrations to make their way towards the cryolab, the English changing rooms, across the corridor, were silent.

A different bounce, more weight on a tackle or a breath of wind and it could have been them singing in celebration. The margins of modern rugby are ever tighter, and ever more cruel because of that. But that is also what energises the game. For the Welsh fans Scott's try provided the kind of moment for which every rugby enthusiast hopes. A moment when the emotional contours of thousands move in exact alignment, switchbacking in just seven seconds from the anxiety of an English attack to the sudden jubilation of Scott's kick through and score. The surprise conjured from the unexpected, the breaking of the pattern that makes the pattern more beautiful, the moment of chance that falls your way. To experience this jeopardy, to be at the mercy of the sport's vagaries, is why we watch rugby. To care and to feel. To experience those moments of play which, as Seamus Heaney says in his poem 'Postscript', *catch the heart off guard and blow it open.*

What a spectator sees as a moment of chance, however, from the perspective of a player or a coach is rarely just chance. Even moments of luck need to be built upon dedication to become winning moments of luck. For Scott it was chance that Jamie Roberts was injured and he took the field, but everything else about his try was the leading edge of a life in which from a young age he'd only ever wanted to play rugby. Watching his stepfather play for Neath on the TV, the hours of skills coaching he'd received at the hands of the Scarlets' Eifion Roberts,

Shaun's defensive drills in which the squad had practised, again and again, ripping the ball from an opponent's arms – all of these, too, were ingredients in those seven seconds in which Scott scored. As Jenks often says, paraphrasing the golfer Jerry Barber, 'the harder you work, the luckier you get'.

With his match-winning try at Twickenham, Scott, at twenty-one, had achieved what most players chase throughout their international careers: the iconic moment which, no matter what else happens, no one can take away from you. The moment for which you will be remembered. With that try he's already answered the banner in the Barn which asks, *How do you want to be remembered?* And he's questioned, too, that other banner next to it – *Yesterday is in the past.* Because as a rugby player, if your past happens to include a seven seconds like Scott's at Twickenham that clear February afternoon, then a part of it, seven seconds of it, will always be in your present too.

'Go on! Guess! She was in *Sister Act 2*. You'll know her, you will!'

The Wales changing rooms in which J.R. has been working alone have begun to fill with other members of the Wales staff making their own preparations for the arrival of the team. Ryan Chambers, the squad's sports scientist, is checking the protein shakes. At an away fixture this is the time when Ryan would usually be preparing the GPS pack each player wears between their shoulder blades in training and during a game. From these he's able to study the players' movements on the pitch, their distances, their speeds and even the momentum and angle of their tackles. In the Millennium Stadium, however, the overhang of the stands blocks the satellite signal, denying Wales this technology at home.

Along from Ryan, Carcass is in the physio area preparing his strapping station, while Prof. John is organising his pitch-side medical equipment. Meanwhile, Ben, the team photographer, is being harried by J.R. to guess the singer playing on the iPod dock.

'Whoopi Goldberg?' Ben says, already unsure of his answer.

'No!' J.R. exclaims, as if a child should have known. 'Lauryn Hill! She was in the film, she was! *Sister Act 2*.'

As Ben and J.R. continue talking, J.R. snapping the players' name plates into the clips above their stalls, Geraint, a member of the stadium's security staff, takes up his position outside the rear doors of the changing room. Opposite him is the VIP lift which the suited coaches, each wearing a daffodil in their lapel, will hurry into after the anthems, frowning and unsmiling, to travel up to the box from where they'll watch the match. At Geraint's back are the double doors into the changing room, through which Ben and J.R.'s muffled voices reach him, the latest in a growing chorus of voices Geraint has heard spreading through the stadium for the last two hours. To Geraint, standing in that windowless corridor on his own, the whole building feels like a stadium-sized battery, charging with anticipation and nerves and excitement, every minute gone and every minute to come transfigured in relation to the 885th minute of the day, when the referee will finally blow his whistle and Wales's last match of the Six Nations will begin.

From here, though, outside the back door of the changing room, Geraint will see none of what happens after that minute. Even the roars of the crowd will be faint this deep in the stadium. He will hear the team return at half-time, and he will, perhaps, hear some of the words spoken to them by the coaches. But then they'll leave again, the clacking of their studs diminishing down the corridor towards the tunnel and the pitch.

When the game is over, they'll return once more, and only then, as Geraint listens from this side of the door either to celebratory music or to silence, will he know if Wales have lost or won.

The streets of Cardiff are filling. The bright morning is still laced with winter but, with the sun's warmth and a rainbow arcing above the walls of Cardiff Castle, it holds the promise of spring too. Roger Lewis, a cup of Costa coffee in one hand, his smartphone in the other, has left the stadium to walk through the city to witness a twelfth of the country's population pour into its centre. Having finished his pitch-side interviews he called in on the changing rooms to see J.R. and the others, before making his way out of the stadium. At Gwyn's security lodge he stopped for a moment to talk with Ryan Jones's father, Steve, who has been walking his three-year-old grandson, Jacob, down the ramped entranceway at Gate 4.

Ryan, at thirty-one, is one of the senior Welsh players. Although much has been made about the youth of the squad this year, it is still veined with a vital steadying seam of experience too. More than once during this campaign Ryan has come off the bench and, like a battle-hardened sergeant, brought a level-headed focus to the forward play, apparently finding, as the more capped players often do, an extra second with which to make his decision or move. As an ex-captain of Wales who has since had to play under others, and with two Grand Slams already to his name, Ryan and his family have, over the last eight years, been through most of the highs and lows that international rugby can throw at a player. If Wales win today, however, then Jacob will see his father reach a new peak, joining a select group of only five other Welshmen to have ever played in three Grand Slams. For Ryan's own father, meanwhile, it will mark the pinnacle of a long journey, one which began many years before Ryan was born, with his own boyhood dreams of one day putting on the red shirt of Wales.

As Roger makes his way up St Mary's, a river of rugby fans flows against him, the Welsh and the French patterning the street with reds and blues from side to side. Stalls selling scarves, flags and hats occasionally break the flow, as does the odd ticket tout standing motionless beside a lamp post, threading their repeated offer into the cacophony of the crowd. 'Buy or sell tickets! Buy or sell tickets!' Their prices, at this hour, are well into three figures.

Because of its cathedral-like position at the centre of the city, an international match in the Millennium Stadium triggers an intensification of Cardiff's population, rather than a dispersal. Like a roosting starling murmur tightening on the wind above a wood, so Wales contracts about the stadium on a match day. While a shopper on Oxford Street in London or on the Royal Mile in Edinburgh might be completely unaware of a rugby match at Twickenham or Murrayfield, it's impossible to be on the streets of the Welsh capital and not know that a game is being played in its stadium. From early morning until late at night the resonance of those eighty minutes electrify the city. The streets pulse with an ever-inward movement as trains and buses from across the country bring the stadium's crowd into Cardiff. Some will travel for hours to get here. The extra carriages added on the trains from the valleys, from Swansea and Bridgend, from Abergavenny and Cwmbran, will develop a spreading virus of red with every hour nearer the game. Today many of those arriving on them will not even have tickets to get inside the stadium. But they still want to be here, to watch on giant screens in the civic areas and in pubs and clubs, to be within sound and sight of the arena where it, whatever it may be, will happen. They want to be here to drink, to share and to feel themselves more than themselves, as if by being closer to the stadium they are somehow closer to an idea of Wales.

In her poem 'Toast', Sheenagh Pugh describes the recently built Millennium Stadium as

> a mother-ship that seems to have landed
> awkwardly in our midst.

And she's right, there is something imposing and 'landed' about the way the stadium sits within Cardiff, its jointed masts angling their Concorde-like tips into previously unoccupied slips and pockets of air. While its West Stand floats above the river, its South abuts challengingly up against office blocks, the joint of the south-eastern mast protruding above Park Street like the prow of a ship. Viewed from further away, from the hills of Fairwater or the Grangetown link road, there is something kinetic about those jointed masts, as if at any moment the whole stadium might lift itself on them and, like a giant insect, scuttle away. At closer quarters, with the sun behind them, those skeletal masts seem to aspire towards spires, as if the stadium would make a claim beyond its location upon the spiritual needs of those who congregate within its stands.

As Roger makes a left into the crowds on Caroline Street, where drinkers are already spilling out of the Brewery Quarter, a woman in a red cowboy hat passes him wearing a T-shirt several sizes too small, its slogan printed across her chest: 'Welsh Lamb @ the Grand Slam'. Further on down the street a Frenchman in a beret is having his cheeks painted with the colours of his flag. A group of boys from the Rhondda look on, all wearing dark wigs of white-bandaged curls in homage to Mervyn Davies, the great Welsh number eight who died yesterday.

For Roger the experience of this morning's stroll is something like that of a director walking through his audience before they enter the theatre to see his play. No one recognises him as he makes his way down Caroline Street and turns left onto the Hayes. And yet, in no small way, this day for which these people have come into the city is Roger's creation. As such, it is also the consequence of another match Wales played forty-six years earlier, when, as a twelve-year-old, Roger boarded a Brownings bus chartered by Cefn Cribwr RFC and travelled into Cardiff to watch Wales against Australia. Standing in the West Terrace of the Arms Park that day Roger had watched Gerald Davies, Barry John and Delme Thomas all make their debuts for Wales. Wales lost 11–14, but for Roger the match lit a passion for Welsh rugby, a passion which would, eventually, lead him to taking this walk today through a match-hyped Hayes as the CEO of the Welsh Rugby Union, on the brink of a game in which, as the Blims sang in the stadium, 'We all hope Wales wins the Grand Slam.'

Every modern rugby union has two hearts: the players and the business. Neither can keep beating without the rhythm of the other. However disparate their worlds might be, success is rarely achieved without embracing the symbiotic relationship between the two. What happens on the pitch fuels the boardroom, and what happens in the boardroom fuels events on the pitch. Roger plays no part in the selection of the players or in their efforts on the field, in the tactics or methods of the coaches or in the medical practices which keep the squad at strength. But just as Warren has spent the last five years building up a team of players and coaches, so Roger, as CEO, has spent the same period building up his own backroom team to help lift the fortunes, both playing and financial, of the WRU. In his own way, within his own field, Roger has enabled today to happen, even though he was never meant to.

Rugby had always been Roger's escape, not his career; a hinterland away from his work. His childhood home in Cefn Cribwr had looked over the village rugby pitch on Mynydd Bach, but he never played for the club. Similarly, at the local Cynffig Comprehensive, it was music, not rugby, that caught Roger's attention. He played at wing-forward in the sixth form, and again as a scrum-half at Nottingham University, but from the end of his education music became his career and rugby its soundtrack, a private pleasure not to be mixed with business.

Roger's first organisational role within a rugby club was as chair of a group overseeing the under-9s at Maidenhead RFC. His two sons had begun playing mini-rugby, so from 1993, for the next ten years, Roger became increasingly involved in the club, coaching, organising tours and heading up committees for certain age groups. Having worked as a composer, musician, head of music for Radio 1 and managing director of the classical division of EMI Records, Roger was then worldwide president of Decca. His schedule, however, was always made to revolve around the Sunday mini-rugby matches back in Maidenhead, even if that meant flying in from New York on a Saturday and leaving for Italy on the Monday. Rugby, through his sons, was moving closer to the centre of Roger's life. But when they grew up, and Roger and his wife Chris moved back to St Hilary in the Vale of Glamorgan, it ebbed away again. Roger had debentures for the new Millennium Stadium and watched Wales play whenever he could, but he still had no idea about the internal dynamics or politics of the professional game.

Three years later, in 2007, Roger was walking into the middle of the pitch at Stade de la Beaujoire at the Rugby World Cup in France, discussing with Dai Pickering, chairman of the WRU, how best to sack the coach of Wales, Gareth Jenkins. The two men were looking for somewhere secluded where they could talk urgently. The match against Fiji was only just over. The stands were still full of celebrating Fijian supporters and devastated Welsh. The middle of the pitch was the most public place in sight, but as somewhere they couldn't be overheard, it was also the most private.

Wales had just been knocked out in the pool stages by Fiji, beaten 38–34. They'd played an open game of running rugby, and in doing so had played into the Fijians' hands. For the first time ever Wales were going home without reaching the quarter-finals. As Roger and Dai walked out into the centre of the pitch, they approached the Fijian players, who were gathered in a huddle, praying. Many of them were crying. As Roger walked past them he recognised that Wales hadn't just lost the game, but something else too, something the Fijians still had. A fundamental spirit within the team's culture had died, and their values and beliefs had been shaken. As a viewer writing into the BBC's website put it, 'Something is rotten in the Welsh camp.' Roger knew that he and the WRU board had to act, and they had to act quickly.

John Williams, the WRU head of communications, joined them in the centre of the pitch and, after a brief discussion, the three men decided they had to send an immediate and unequivocal message to the rugby world. From this moment Wales was changing, starting over. Gathering the other board members, they called an extraordinary board meeting in the corner of the stadium, where it was agreed by fifteen to one that the Welsh coach, Gareth Jenkins, had to go. In twenty matches in charge of Wales he'd won only six. He'd inherited a squad still reeling from the resignation of their previous coach, Mike Ruddock. But he'd also asked the country to judge him on his performance at the World Cup. That judgement, as Roger and the board members left the stadium, was already coming in, from newspaper articles, from TV pundits and from fans on rugby websites and forums.

The next day Roger addressed the entire squad, dressed in their number ones – team suits and ties – at their camp outside Nantes. He'd already spoken with Gareth Jenkins and asked him to resign. When he'd refused, Roger told him he was no longer the coach of Wales. Which is what he also told the squad standing before him that day. 'The process of rebuilding', he said, 'begins now.'

In interviews later that week Roger would use Oliver Cromwell's phrase about the execution of King Charles I – 'a cruel necessity' – to describe the sacking of Jenkins. It was undoubtedly just that. But it was also a massive risk. Once that necessity had been taken care of, Wales, just four months away from the 2008 Six Nations, were without a coach.

It was the resignation of one Wales coach, Mike Ruddock on 14 February 2006, that had set Roger on the path to being the man who would fire another a year later in Nantes. Listening to the breaking news reports of Ruddock's departure in his kitchen at St Hilary that day, it was clear to Roger, even from a distance, that the WRU had become 'a distressed organisation', in disarray both on and off the field. He recognised the scent of that disarray from having smelt it himself in other companies in which he'd worked. But on Valentine's Day 2006, as he listened to reports about the disintegration of the WRU, Roger still had no idea he'd ever be involved in picking up the pieces.

That summer the job of CEO of the Welsh Rugby Union was advertised in the *Sunday Times*. Roger was approached to apply shortly afterwards, and it was then, as he considered the role, that he realised perhaps elements of his experience in the music industry may be transferable to the modern game of professional rugby. Both worlds, however different, were about dealing with elite performers – *singers and players, producers and coaches* – who provide content – *teams and bands, songs and matches* – which needs to be delivered through various mechanisms – *venues and stadia, TV and media* – and monetised – *through audience and spectators, sponsors and merchandise*. Just as in music, rugby had its elite and its grassroots concerns, each feeding the other. Roger had overseen the development of elite musicians often from their youth, from the same kind of ages as rugby players. Modern rugby was increasingly about entertainment and performance, about handling talent and harnessing passion, both in the players and the fans. Viewed from this perspective, Roger saw no reason why the lessons he'd learnt in studios and concert halls shouldn't be applied to the training pitch and the rugby field; why his private interest shouldn't become a public role.

One of the lessons Roger had learnt was that if you're chasing the best producer or the best artist, you turn up. You don't ask them into your office, but get on a plane and meet them backstage. You hang out with them. Which is why, within weeks of addressing the squad in Nantes, Roger, Dai Pickering and Gerald Davies, the three-man delegation tasked with finding a new coach for Wales, landed in an airport on the other side of the world.

In their initial research, speaking to coaches, players and commentators, it had become clear to the team that they would have to look beyond the UK for their candidates. Certain names kept cropping up, and nearly all of them were from the only other country whose national obsession with the sport rivalled Wales's: New Zealand.

To an extent Roger, Dai and Gerald were looking for a quality of character as much as a coach. This was a search bound up with questions of national identity. When

Roger had come into the WRU, he'd articulated a vision for the organisation that, tellingly, was couched in terms of self-expression and nation-building. 'The WRU', he said, 'will take Wales to the world and, in our stadium, will welcome the world to Wales. Together we will play our part in defining Wales as a nation.'

And yet in their meetings in New Zealand Roger and the others would be considering foreign coaches, men who hadn't grown up with the ethos of Wales running in their veins, to carry the precious but fragile vase that is the hopes of Welsh rugby. Whoever took on the position would need to have an innate empathy for Wales beyond national association. The WRU badly needed an outsider's eye and influence, but they also needed that crucial note of understanding; a stranger attuned to the nature of the country's culture, but who could also be clear-sighted about her qualities, good and bad.

Within twenty minutes of meeting Warren Gatland at Auckland airport Roger felt they'd found the next coach of Wales. There was something about Warren's blend of emotional intelligence and blue-collar background that sounded the right note. He was also realistic, pragmatic and straight-talking, capable of detaching himself from the romance that both bolsters and hinders so much Welsh support for the national side.

Warren would meet some of that passionate support on his first night in Wales, when he came to stay with Roger at St Hilary. On taking him into his local pub,

The Bush, Roger was in conversation with Warren when a man approached from the bar and tapped Warren on the shoulder. 'Excuse me, Mr Gatland,' he said. 'I'd like to introduce myself. I'm one of the 2.9 million selectors in Wales. Good luck.'

It was a well-intentioned but premature gesture. Despite speculation in the media, Warren hadn't yet accepted the position of Wales head coach, and Roger had yet to formally ask him. He had, instead, invited Warren to Wales to 'just talk', and to give him an opportunity to witness first hand the position rugby occupied within the country's psyche and landscape.

The following morning, by way of beginning this process, Roger chartered a helicopter from Cardiff bay and flew Warren across South Wales, allowing the New Zealander to get a proper look at his prospective employer from the air. From Cardiff, following Roger's instructions, the pilot flew along the southern corridor of Welsh rugby's heartland. Tracking the unspooling M4, they passed over Newport, the ground at Rodney Parade and the Gwent valleys. Below them the long villages and towns of South Wales bled into each other, their roofs and streets frequently punctuated with the green of rugby pitches. Beyond their borders these towns gave way to hedged farmland or barren hillsides grazed by wild ponies. 'It looks like New Zealand,' Warren said, looking out of his window at the land spread below him. Turning west over Ebbw Vale they flew around the sculpted peaks of Pen y

Fan and the Beacons before dropping south over Rhigos and heading further west to Stradey Park in Llanelli, then over the building works of Parc y Scarlets, Rhossili Bay and around the peninsula of Worms Head. Heading back east the helicopter flew over Swansea and the city's new Liberty Stadium and the ground at St Helen's where Warren had once played. Taking in the Gnoll at Neath and the Brewery Field in Bridgend, they finally returned to Cardiff, making a pass over the Millennium Stadium and the pitch which would, if Warren accepted the job, be his new home ground.

But Roger didn't want the tour to end there. Having landed, they got into his two-seater Mercedes and drove up into the Rhondda, through Tylorstown and Treorchy, before passing through the Bwlch and down the Ogmore valley to his mother's house in Cefn Cribwr, where Roger suggested they stop for some tea. As Roger stepped inside the small terraced house that was his childhood home, he introduced Warren to his eighty-one-year-old mother. 'I know who he is!' she admonished her son in reply, before turning back to Warren. 'Now,' she said, taking his hand and leading him into the living room, 'what you going to do about Gavin Henson?'

As Roger emerges back onto Westgate Street, the Millennium Stadium rears into view. The first fans are beginning to enter the building, flowing up to the gates in steady streams. Others are already taking up their positions on the corner of the street outside the Angel Hotel or along the castle walls, ready to welcome the arrival of the Wales team bus into the city. All of Cardiff is engaged in a single conversation, the crowds bonded by a shared anticipation. A group of French supporters pose for photographs with a mounted policeman. A young woman in high heels and a mini-dress pauses beside them to stroke the horse's neck, her gold sequinned handbag swinging from her shoulder. From further down the street a hooter sounds. Another replies. Outside Gate 3 an S4C TV crew are interviewing the welsh boxer, Joe Calzaghe, asking him for his prediction on the match. 'Wales will win,' Joe says, 'but it'll be close.'

Looking over Joe's interview is a statue of the late Sir Tasker Watkins, once deputy Lord Chief Justice and ex-president of the Welsh Rugby Union. In a couple of hours' time the tide of spectators will have risen even further, with thousands flowing up the incline of Gate 3 to maroon the bespectacled Sir Tasker, his hands behind his back, in a sea of red and blue.

As an officer serving with the Welsh Regiment in the

Second World War, Sir Tasker was awarded a VC for leading his men in a bayonet charge in Normandy. When Graham Henry was Wales coach, he sometimes pinned Sir Tasker's citation in the team's changing room before a Six Nations match:

On 16 August 1944 at Barfour, Normandy, France, Lieutenant Watkins' company came under murderous machine-gun fire while advancing through corn fields set with booby traps. The only officer left, Lieutenant Watkins led a bayonet charge with his 30 remaining men against 50 enemy infantry, practically wiping them out. Finally, at dusk, separated from the rest of the battalion, he ordered his men to scatter and after he had personally charged and silenced an enemy machine-gun post, he brought them back to safety. His superb leadership not only saved his men, but decisively influenced the course of the battle.

Roger walks on towards the stadium. Once inside he'll take the VIP lift up to the President's Lounge on level five, where he'll begin welcoming over a hundred guests for the pre-match lunch. These will include members of the Fédération Française de Rugby, the first minister of Wales, Carwyn Jones, ex-players, politicians, sponsors, business people, academics and broadcasters. A team of young men and women will take coats, hanging them on two long racks on either side of the door into the lounge. Once inside waiters and waitresses will greet the guests with trays of red and white wine, while others circulate with canapés. A bar will serve beer and gin and tonics. The room itself, with its bank of windows looking out over the County Club and the city, will be charged with a heightened sense of being, like the Blims on the pitch this morning, at the centre of the centre.

Once his guests are seated, Dennis Gethin, the president of the WRU, will address the room first in Welsh, then in French and finally, 'for the less civilised among us', in English. His introductory speech over and grace recited, the starters will be served and everyone will begin to eat and drink, to drink and eat, laying napkins over protruding stomachs or across the hems of delicate dresses. The whole lounge, five floors above the changing rooms where Carcass is preparing his strapping station, where Ryan mixes the rehydration drinks and Prof. John is checking his needles and thread, feasts, drinks and talks, celebrating together before the game begins.

And in the sponsors' boxes around the stadium, too, meals are being served and drinks are being poured. And in the bars on level three the 'joy machines' are already pumping out twelve pints at a time. And in the family rooms and the ex-players' lounge those who are closest to the squad and those who have been here before them eat and drink, drink and eat. The whole stadium, from top to bottom, apart from those two quiet changing rooms either side of the tunnel, is loud with expectation, occasion and alcohol.

Inside the jacket pockets of the men and in the handbags of the women dining in the President's Lounge long WRU wallets hold their other invitations for the day: for post-match tea, and later to the black-tie post-match dinner at the Hilton. On each glossy invitation is the image of a Welsh rugby shirt, its fabric and feathers filled out by the chest and shoulders of a player, their head cropped off at the base of the neck.

## 12 p.m.

Twelve miles further west a quieter pre-match lunch is coming to an end in the Wales team room at the Vale. The remaining players at the tables are silent, occupied in thought. Leigh Halfpenny is still nervous. As much as possible he will not talk to anyone before the match, or smile. The eighty minutes of the game, everything for which they have trained, is almost upon them. The whole team know how the story is meant to go today, and each player has rehearsed his role in its performance. But they also all remember their last game against France; how it got away from them, and in so doing, wrote them out of the World Cup final.

Sam, their captain who watched that match slip away from the sidelines, is finding it difficult to eat. Twelve miles away the Millennium Stadium is already filling with 75,000 spectators. Two hundred and fifty thousand people are on the streets of Cardiff. The bars of the pubs are three deep with drinkers. The build-up to the match has been on TV and radio all day. Images of Sam and the squad are all over the newspapers. Children across Wales have woken and put on Wales rugby shirts. Not that long ago, he was a child himself, telling his mother from his pillow he'd never be a rugby player. Today he is a rugby player. Today he will captain his country. Sam looks down at his plate and, for that child and for his country, spears another piece of chicken and eats.

Two floors above the team room, Thumper Phillips, the Wales team manager, is getting into his number ones. Standing before the mirror in his room he loops a WRU tie about his neck, constructs a knot and pulls it tight before flipping down the collar of his shirt. Lifting his jacket off a hanger, he puts it on and, leaning into the mirror so he can see better, pins a daffodil to his lapel.

At fifty-eight Thumper is the same age as Roger Lewis and was brought up in the same part of Wales too, in Kenfig Hill, half a mile down the road from where Roger took Warren for tea with his mother. The two men have known each other since they were twelve, when they first met on the playground of the local comprehensive. On leaving school they took diverging paths in life, but both, eventually, have led them back into close proximity, working either side of that relationship between the business and the players that lies at the heart of the WRU.

It was Thumper's uncle, Alan, who first took his nephew to the midweek Floodlight Alliance games at Maesteg and the Brewery Field in Bridgend. On those dark Wednesday nights the ten-year-old Thumper watched enthralled as the likes of Gareth Edwards and Phil Bennett played to capacity crowds. Already showing promise as a player himself, within another ten years it was Thumper who was running onto those pitches instead, having been selected for Cardiff directly from the Kenfig Hill youth team.

A few weeks before he first played for Cardiff, Thumper was walking back from training in Kenfig Hill to his home in Pyle when a car pulled up and its driver asked him if he knew where he could find Alan Phillips. Thumper said he did, and that if the driver gave him a lift into the village he'd show him where he lived. As they drove into Pyle the man introduced himself as Gary Davies of Cardiff RFC. He asked Thumper how he knew Alan Phillips. 'Because', Thumper replied, 'I am Alan Phillips.'

Along with Roy Bish, Gary had recently watched Thumper score all his team's points in a 24–12 victory over Llanelli. Within a week of having stopped him to ask him where he could find Alan Phillips, Gary had Thumper training with Cardiff. Within another week he was playing for them too, thumbing lifts into training from Pyle after work and getting dropped off back in Bridgend by Gary afterwards. Sixteen years later, at the age of thirty-four, Thumper retired, having played more games for Cardiff than any other player in the club's history, earning himself eighteen Welsh caps and a 1980 Lions tour to South Africa along the way.

Today, as Wales team manager, Thumper finds himself overseeing boys young enough to be his grandsons who, he says, 'play a totally different game' to the one he knew when he was making his way at their age. As Thumper often says, 'Only the shape of the ball is the same now.' The changes have mostly been driven by professionalism, but also by changes in the rules around the contact area and a gradual eradication of the hard-man culture that in Thumper's day rarely saw a clean game of rugby.

'I played in a period when there were no touch judges, nothing like that, when people were punching from behind, running across the field when you least expected it. It was a dirty game, a dirty game. But no one ever got hurt, mind, not really hurt. A few broken jaws maybe, that kind of thing.'

The current players, though, don't necessarily have it any easier. 'You couldn't get away with that now, you *have* to respect the rules of the game. But it is physically tougher,' Thumper admits. 'The boys are quicker, more powerful. I mean, I was fourteen and a half stone as a hooker. Matthew Rees is seventeen and a half, three stone heavier. Ken Owens, Hibs, they're big men, big men. There's less time, everyone's under analysis. It's hard.'

Possessed of a quartermaster's manner, Thumper carries out his duties with the same confrontational style he once brought to his forward play. With a restless pointing finger, often addressing people from over his glasses, and his signature black satchel cross-gartered over his chest, Thumper is a man who wants to solve problems, and who is confident in his ability to do so. His diplomacy is direct and frequently followed by the effective technique of walking away before a counterpoint can be made. It is often, too, edged with sharp humour. While on tour to Canada Thumper christened one of the team's liaison officers 'Thrush', 'because he was an irritating little cunt'.

Beneath Thumper's organisational bluster is a deep well of care, both for the individual players and for the game of rugby itself. 'It's a great game to protect,' he says. 'It teaches you respect by bashing the shit out of each other, but you also have to respect the rules. But you've gotta protect it, its traditions, because if you lose them, then you lose the respect of the game, and without that', he adds, shaking his head at the worst possible fate, 'we'd be like football.'

One of Thumper's most persistent challenges as team manager is satisfying the increasing demands of marketing and PR upon the squad, while still protecting the team they are trying to promote. In this respect Thumper sees himself as a buffer between the team and the world; an old-fashioned gatekeeper at the heart of a twenty-first-century squad. It's his job, he says, to be the 'awkward bugger', to try and defend what sacred time and space the team still own. The words he uses most often when talking about this element of his role are 'tradition' and 'respect'. In the face of an ever-increasing appetite for access to the players, the erosion of these qualities is what most concerns Thumper. 'I mean,' he says, 'everyone can buy our kit now. Anyone. We have changing-room visits by sponsors after a game. These kids in marketing, they want to show more and more of us, give more and more of us away. I understand why it has to happen, but you got to keep something back, haven't you? Otherwise what you got left?'

Not that Thumper would ever want the team to withdraw from their fans. On the contrary, he sees the players as 'ambassadors for Wales. How we act and conduct ourselves reflects on the people of Wales.' To this end Thumper takes a gruff paternal interest in the manners of the younger players. 'I tell them to keep their feet off the tables, how to eat at dinner, that kind of thing. And I always tell them to have time for the supporters too, be well-mannered, y'know? Because people are looking at these boys and they're dreaming, aren't they? When they look at them,' Thumper says, beginning to walk away, 'these people, when they see them, they're seeing their dreams.'

## The Journey

### 1 p.m.

Sounding its horn five times in acknowledgement, the dragon-painted team bus of Wales pulls away from the kerb outside the Vale as the crowd of fans gathered behind orange barriers wave and cheer it on its way. As a police motorcycle escorts it onto the resort's exit road, more fans are standing in the car park, cameras held before their faces in one hand, waving with the other. From behind the bus the applause and cheers outside the Vale continue.

On board, however, it is silent.

Thumper, his black satchel on his lap, sits at the front of the bus behind the driver. Warren sits in the other front seat, across the aisle. Behind them are the rest of the coaches: Rob Howley, Rob McBryde, Adam, Dan and Shaun. Behind them again the players of the squad have taken up a pair of seats each. Dressed in identical red tracksuits, many of them wearing headphones, they sit along the length of both sets of windows, their kitbags beside them. No one talks. Ahead of them, through the driver's windscreen, a second police motorcycle escort has joined the convoy. The motorbikes lead them on through the golf-course grounds of the Vale. An approaching white Rolls-Royce, decked in pink ribbon, slows up and pulls over to let them pass. As they do, the bride and her father inside wave, and the chauffeur sounds his horn.

The bus drives on, shuddering over a cattle grid and turning left up a hedged country lane towards the M4. As it reaches a roundabout the only sounds are its engine, climbing and falling through the gears, and the faint beat of dance tracks leaking from headphones. Adam Beard, sitting towards the front of the bus, thinks he can hear the heartbeat of Ryan Jones, sitting behind him.

The bus takes the roundabout and drops down onto the M4 heading east, towards Cardiff. Still no one on board talks. And no one will, all the way into the stadium, this being one of the team's most established match-day traditions. The bus, usually a place of banter and joking, on this journey becoming something else: a vehicle of transition, in which the men inside will go from being a group of players to becoming, in twelve miles' time, Wales.

In this moment the twenty-two members of the squad are both together and not. They are all on the same bus, travelling to the same destination, and yet they are also in twenty-two different worlds, listening to different songs and thinking about different people and pasts. But with every mile closer to the city they are a mile closer to shedding their separation, a mile closer to those eighty minutes when they will exist, instead, as a team. A fifteen-headed animal which will try, in the heat of a game and under the eyes of millions, to think, react and move as one.

An overtaking car sounds its horn in support, a Welsh scarf flying madly from its open window. There are now four police motorcycles leading the bus, their blue lights rotating, as in the distance the capital of Wales begins to rise into view.

Halfway up the bus on the left-hand side Jamie Roberts is listening to the same song he always plays on this journey: 'Lucky Man' by the Verve. As he has been for all of the Six Nations, Jamie, who at twenty-five is the oldest in Wales's backline, is today's defensive captain. It will be his role to guide the team through Shaun's defensive tactics, to decide when they blitz or drift, to keep an eye on line speed, the splitting of centres and the positioning of the back three. It was, however, as an attacking centre that Jamie made his mark in the Wales set-up, his seventeen stone four pounds providing the coaches with a midfield battering ram to deploy at will.

This season, with the help of Adam Beard, Jamie has increased that penetrative power even more. On taking charge of Wales's physical performance Adam was clear about where his priorities lay, and Jamie was the perfect candidate for his thinking. Adam wanted to develop not just the strength and speed of the team, but also their efficiency, specifically their running economy. As Adam once said to Sam, 'The first thing a water-polo coach will do is train his players to swim properly. What do you spend most of a game doing? Running. But have we been teaching players to run?'

The answer was no, and yet on average a player will run seven or eight kilometres in a match. For Wales, who prefer a high ball-in-play time – around thirty-five minutes – a player's ability to move about the field quickly, to get off the ground, to ruck and chase is even more crucial. As Adam told the players again and again as he pushed them on the frozen beaches of Gdansk, 'We should be the best at everything that doesn't require talent. Effort doesn't require talent. Hard work doesn't require talent. We should be the best at hard work.' And with that, he'd put them through another set of drills, asking them again to work through a level of fatigue they'd never felt before.

From Adam's perspective Wales had been creating big, strong players like Jamie, but not looking closely enough at their movement, at what was required of their bodies in a game. 'We'd been creating these V8 engines', he explains, 'and putting them in shopping trolleys. But I wanted to put them in a Porsche or a Ferrari instead.'

In Jamie's case this meant trimming down his quads, putting more stiffness in the Achilles tendon and strengthening his hamstrings. The result has been to make him not only more efficient, but also faster, increasing the force of his momentum up into the region of George North's one tonne of impact.

Adam has gone through similar processes with all the players on this bus, examining points of strain along their kinetic chains, fine-tuning and adapting their physiques, then working with Dan to find drills and exercises through which to develop new patterns of muscle memory. With players like Toby Faletau, the young Tongan-born number eight from Ebbw Vale, Adam has strengthened certain muscle groups and introduced co-ordination training to bring his anaerobic test scores from down at prop level up to an impressive 130 seconds. In this way, borrowing from eastern European sprint coaches, Australian Rules football and athletics, Adam has moved beyond the formal studies of biomechanics and a purely mechanistic training routine. In doing so, combined with a carefully constructed programme of cryotherapy, he has managed to shift the squad out of those shopping trolleys and into supercars.

Except, of course, this being rugby, each game Wales plays isn't like taking those Porsches and Ferraris for a spin on the track, but more like putting them through the beating of a stock-car race. So the players on this bus have to be Land Rovers as well as Ferraris. And many other equivalent vehicles too. In the course of a single match they'll be expected to run like sprinters, lift like weightlifters, kick with the skill of footballers and endure hits like Ultimate Fighters. All of which means that at some point, however sophisticated the training or the physio, their bodies will break down.

That Jamie is playing at all today is an achievement.

Throughout the campaign he's been carrying a knee injury, and in less than a week's time he'll go under the knife. Somehow, though, Prav and Carcass, working alongside Adam from the other end of the process, have managed to keep Jamie match-fit, as they have the entire Wales starting backline for every match of the tournament. Given the attrition rate of modern rugby, this fact is a feat in itself.

Injury is no longer an 'if' in the modern game, more a 'when' and 'how bad?' No player goes through a season fully fit, and an entire team will often take the field harbouring some kind of an injury. From a young age injury stalks a rugby player, and for many on this bus their careers will be framed by it. At any moment, regardless of how young a player might be, they may unknowingly already be at the peak of their game. Like Dan Baugh, someone else's injury will open a door for them, before one of their own, eventually, will close it again. More than one player in the squad has admitted to thinking about this before each match. 'Will this be the game that ends it? If not, how many more before I play the one that does?'

As a consequence the modern rugby player, while physically robust, inhabits a fragile existence in which they occupy an ever-narrowing space between two uncertainties: the chance of injury and the doubt of selection. The two are interrelated, which is why many of these players never thought they would be on the bus today as it drives on towards Cardiff and a Grand Slam decider against France. For all of them each selection is not only a matter of beating the others vying for your shirt, but also of defying the physical vagaries of the game: the twist, tear, break or dislocation that sees fortunes rise and fall in the turn of a second.

This has certainly been the case for all three second rows on the bus, their heads rising higher over the seats than the other players. At the start of the campaign the towering Luke Charteris, just a few inches off seven foot, still had his wrist in a cast. Alun Wyn Jones was out with 'turf toe', while Ian 'Ianto' Evans, after three years of injuries, considered himself so far out of contention he'd planned his wedding and honeymoon to coincide with the squad's upcoming summer tour of Australia. And yet, in illustration of how drastically a player's week, month or year can change, by the end of today Ianto will be the only Welsh player to have played every second of every match for the whole of the Six Nations. 'You have to play the patience game,' Ianto says, speaking of his years of injury. 'It's like hitting your head against a brick wall until the crack becomes a little bigger, until eventually you can get through it and see beyond it. But mentally it's very tough,' he adds, nodding his head in recollection. 'Very tough.'

Across the aisle from Jamie, and one of the few on the bus not listening to music, is the hooker and ex-captain of Wales, Matthew Rees, or 'Smiler', as he's known to the squad. As his moniker suggests, Matthew's natural expression falls into the suggestion of a quiet, *Mona Lisa*-like smile, as if he's just remembered a joke at which you'll only ever be able to guess. Even now, as he looks out at the cars passing the bus, tooting their horns, the fans giving thumbs up through their windows, the echo of a grin still plays at the corners of his mouth.

Today will be Matthew's fiftieth cap. To mark the occasion he'll lead the team out onto the field. As recently as a few weeks ago, though, Matthew thought he wouldn't be here today. Having already missed the 2011 World Cup with a neck injury, he recovered, only to tear his calf muscle in training before the Ireland match, meaning he would miss the first three games of the tournament. 'It was', he says, 'hard, very hard. The lowest point in my career.'

Matthew was part of the 2007 World Cup squad when an underprepared Wales underperformed and were knocked out by Fiji. So to go through the hardships of Poland, to feel the 'sense of belief' in this squad, knowing they'd trained harder than ever before, and then not to be able to join them was heartbreaking for Matthew, and even more so because he knew he'd lose the captaincy to Sam in the process. At the start of the Six Nations, after he injured his calf, it looked as if he'd have to experience the same again: to train with a squad hungry for the Grand Slam, and yet not be part of it. His only hope, as all players know, was to give his all in rehab, which he did, working all hours of the day and night with Carcass to try and win back his place in the team.

'Rehab' is a word often used when talking about rugby players, but one that is strangely dislocated from the reality of its meaning. Only those who have undergone the million shoulder rotations, or the all-night, two-hourly icing of a thigh, or the endless repetition of the same stretch or single exercise will know that rehab is, in many ways, a tougher ordeal than regular training. Most of it is done alone, without a team beside you. And all of it is done in hope, not certainty. At the end, even if you are successful and return to full fitness, there is no guarantee another player hasn't already staked a claim to your shirt in your absence. But however hard it is, rehab is also a truth of the modern game, the unseen struggle every player undergoes at some point in their career. Which is why, as the Wales bus continues down the M4 towards Cardiff, along with the players inside, it also bears their thousands of hours of rehab, as much a part of this team as their years of playing and training on the pitch.

Even without injury, from the longer perspective of his childhood Matthew never imagined he'd one day be on this bus, travelling towards his fiftieth cap. Although as a child he was an avid rugby fan, rushing out to play in the street after watching Wales on TV, coming from Tonyrefail in the Rhondda Matthew didn't think international players came from places like his valley, his home. That he began to think they might, and that he could be one of them, was down to one man: Chris Jones, the coach of Rhondda schools. It was Chris who gave the eleven-year-old Matthew a sense of belief, who opened the possibility for him that perhaps, just perhaps, if he worked hard enough, he could make that journey from playing on the streets of the Rhondda to playing on the national ground in Cardiff. Which, fifteen years later at the age of twenty-six, he did, running out at the Millennium Stadium against Australia in 2006.

Such is the brevity of a rugby generation that today's bus is able to contain not just Matthew's achievement but also, in Jenks sitting a few rows in front of him, the symbol of his boyhood aspiration. When Matthew went out onto those streets as a kid to chuck a ball around, he and his mates would choose which Welsh players they'd like to be. Matthew always chose to be Neil Jenkins, Wales's outside-half points machine. Within a few years he found himself rooming with Jenks, when they both played for Pontypridd. Now, as player and coach, they are both on this bus, members of the same Wales squad. And yet to this day Matthew has never told Jenks that when as a boy he'd dreamed of playing for Wales, it was through him that he did so. Jenks who, like Chris Jones, has had a hand in developing the talents and aspirations of so many young players, Matthew Rees, even if he still doesn't know it, being one of them.

All the players on this bus have coaches like Chris

Jones in their past: the friend's father who volunteered at their mini-rugby games, the school PE teacher, the coach of their junior, youth or local sides. The coaches who put in the hours when these men were boys, who first lit their touchpapers of hope and enthusiasm. Or it may have been someone later in their development: a regional skills or defence coach, or the head of strength and conditioning. Whoever it was, they took their game to the next level, spent time with them, passing on knowledge and advice, pushing them further and making them believe.

Whoever these men are, they too, along with the squad's thousands of hours of training and rehab, are travelling on this bus into Cardiff today. As each player boarded at the Vale, they carried the influences of these men onto the coach with them. And they carried on, too, the memories of the hundreds of pitches and playing fields across the country on which they learnt their craft. In Risca, Bancyfelin, Abercrave, Carmarthen, Llandeilo, Rhayader, Gorseinon, Tonyrefail, Aberavon, Llangefni, St Clears. On pitches levelled out of high valleys like Aztec terraces; or on West Walian farming fields, scattered with dandelion and thick with clover; or on school pitches with turf worn away by the patterns of other sports. As the bus takes a slip road off the motorway and drops towards the capital, these fields and places of Wales, with their *tir* and their *pridd*, are also freighted on this coach; distinct yet shared echoes in each player's past as they make their way towards today's match and its eighty minutes of heightened present.

A few seats along from Matthew, Leigh, looking out at the passing buildings, is listening to a song by the Foo Fighters; then, as the bus is guided through a set of traffic lights by its escort, a dance track he's copied from Gethin Jenkins. Jonathan Davies sits opposite him, looking out at the passing shops, parks and trees. Like Matthew he doesn't wear headphones. He used to have a match-day playlist for this journey, but he's stopped that now. Keeping things simple has become Jon's mantra for a match day instead. Keeping it calm and simple.

Alun Wyn Jones is also choosing to keep it calm, listening to the languid songs of Ben Howard. When he was younger he wanted heavy stuff – rock and dance – but with experience he's learnt not to stoke his emotions too soon. Like the rest of the squad he'll be spending the next two hours trying to reach the right balance between aggression and focus, between adrenalin and nerves. At the moment, as the bus moves through Cardiff, that balance is still weighted more towards nerves. But this is how he likes it at this stage in the day. If he isn't nervous now, with the stadium just minutes away, then that's when Alun Wyn becomes fearful, worried he's become too complacent, too accepting. But this, the bubbling of anticipation under the skin, the blend of foreknowledge and the unknown, the gradual building of internal energy, these are the kind of nerves that work for Alun Wyn and which will, he hopes, provide the tinder to fire him when he takes to the pitch.

The bus drives on, the fizz and beat from leaking headphones still the only sound. With four miles to go they are over halfway. The more experienced players have an idea of what will be waiting for them as they drive deeper into the city. For winger Alex Cuthbert, though, who played his first fifteen-a-side game just this time last year, he only has the stories of those who have already witnessed a Grand Slam with which to try and picture what is waiting for them on the streets of the capital. What he does know for certain, however, is that they are about to break the bubble of their isolation. In four miles' time they will be delivered from their week of preparation in the Vale, from their days of focused and steady training, straight into the heat of a Welsh cauldron of expectation and hope.

For Alex, sitting as he has done for all four previous matches on the right-hand side of the bus, today is the pinnacle of a dizzying ascent to the top of international rugby. It was only four years ago that a coach at Hartbury College spotted him playing a lunchtime game of sevens with some mates. He was playing football for Gloucester City at the time, and while he'd always been into his sports, from athletics, in which he was a forty-nine-second 400m runner, to show jumping, Alex had never properly tried rugby. Within a year of that lunch-time game he was playing for Wales Sevens, and within another two he had a contract with Cardiff Blues and had been called up to the full national squad.

Although Alex is as big and fast as George on the other wing, he is also raw and still learning how to read the game. George has been playing since the age of ten. Others in the squad, such as James Hook or Mike Phillips, have been playing since the age of five. These players have rugby in their veins; the rhythms and patterns of a match are woven into their spatial awareness. Alex, in comparison, is still being shaped with every second on the pitch. What he lacks in experience, however, he more than makes up for with his energy of attack and undying, emotional enthusiasm. When the exertion of a match is starting to show in others, Alex will still be looking for the ball, eager to unleash his coiled speed upon the opposition. As Rob Howley once said of him, referring to both his horse-riding past and his strength and stamina, 'The thing about Cuthbert is, he *is* the fucking horse.'

Although he may have played for more years than Alex, George, sitting a few seats away, still fizzes with equal enthusiasm, no less genuine than the day he came home from his first rugby training session and told his father, 'It's awesome! You can run at people, run around them, and you can tackle them!' During the first Wales match this year, against Ireland in Dublin, George performed all three of those boyhood observations with world-class timing and focus. In the process, he provided a moment of brilliance that became emblematic of Wales's intentions for the tournament.

It happened in the fifty-fourth minute of the game. With Wales trailing by five points George took the ball from Rhys Priestland in midfield to go outside Ireland's D'Arcy before bulldozing the Irish centre McFadden with a massive impact. As he was tackled by another two defenders, George deftly off-loaded the ball to Jonathan Davies with a backwards 'cat-flap' of a pass. The sheer power of his flooring of McFadden drew a gasp from the crowd. It was immediately followed by a cheer of appreciation as he flipped the ball to Jon, who sprinted through the gap to score a vital try under the posts. In creating that gap George had not only taken out four Irish players, but had also displayed a perfect moment of 'beauty and the beast' rugby; an almost simultaneous show of brute strength and delicate skill that had kids across Wales copying his back-handed offload for weeks.

In the changing rooms after the match Warren acknowledged the remarkable disparity between his young winger's age and his performance. 'And to think you're nineteen years old,' he said to George in front of the whole team, shaking his head in disbelief. 'You were world-class out there today.' George, bowing his head, smiled in response.

And yet within the hour, in suit and tie at the

post-match dinner, George's age seemed to have found him once more. As he bounded across to the bar, a Diet Coke disappearing in one huge hand, he looked, despite his height, every inch the sixth-former at a school-leavers' disco, those massive limbs which had done such damage on the pitch imbued once more with a teen-ager's energetic awkwardness. But however young he might have appeared that evening, it was the maturity and finesse of George's play that continued to fire the celebrations. His determination, skill and strength in that single moment quickly became symbolic of Wales's win, its resonance fuelling the Welsh fans' drinking on the streets of Dublin and the smile of Roger Lewis as he played blues and boogie-woogie on the hotel's piano long into the night.

George himself recognises that being thrown into top-flight rugby has accelerated his maturity. 'It's been an intense couple of years,' he says. 'Sometimes it feels as if I left home, grew up, played for Wales, straight one after the other.' Which is, more or less, exactly what happened.

After a year of schoolboy rugby George had just one afternoon off at the end of his exams before starting pre-season training with the Scarlets the next morning. Since then he hasn't stopped through a year with the Scarlets, an autumn international series, a shoulder operation and rehab, more regional rugby and the Six Nations, the World Cup, the European Championship and now the Six Nations once again. With the end of the season and the squad's summer tour still ahead of him, by the time George finally gets a break from rugby in July he will, like many of the players on this bus, have been on a treadmill of playing and training for almost two years.

When George does get that break he'll use much of it to return to his home in North Wales, driving the length of the country to get back to his family on Ynys Môn. For most of the drive there's no phone signal, so, for once, no one can get hold of him. For a few brief hours, listening to music, looking at the views, George is alone as he heads north on the A470 through the mountains of mid-Wales. With each mile he drives, George is aware of an elision occurring in his mind between the length of a rugby pitch and the length of the country, the territory of one mapping over the other. It's an elision he thinks of consciously in his car, acknowledging to himself that each tree, village, hill he passes is another part of the country he represents when he puts on the red shirt of Wales. Today the same thought will come to him again, but more sensed than known when, amid 75,000 voices, he'll experience that eighty-minute contraction when the length of Wales is squeezed into those hundred metres of pitch. 'I come from a small village,' George says. 'But when I play for Wales, I come from a big country.'

For George that feeling is simply the best thing in the world. There is nothing like it. He gets goose pimples just talking about it. And yet exactly because it means so much to George, because representing and winning for

Wales means everything to him, there are times when he has to remember it isn't. That it is, in fact, just a game. This is something sports psychologist Andy McCann has worked on with the young winger. How to switch off away from rugby, in order to prevent, as George puts it, 'the thing you love from killing you'. How to be prepared, but not over-prepared, to think but not over-think. How to treat a game as the most important thing in the world, yet still take the winning or the losing of it in your stride.

For George, most of these questions are answered with a negotiation between remembering and forgetting: forgetting the stresses and import of the game, and remembering the joy he's always got from playing it, ever since he returned from that first training session as an excited ten-year-old. As the bus follows its escort into Cowbridge Road, this is what George reminds himself of again now. To harness the same pleasure for this match as that which he felt when throwing a ball around with his friends on the 'cabbage patch' beside Llangefni Thirds. Which is why, when George is sitting in his stall later, writing trigger words on his strapping, the first word he'll spell out on the inside of his wrist will be 'Enjoy'.

Dan Lydiate, sitting a few seats behind George, has worked with Andy on switching off away from rugby too. But along with Andy's techniques Dan also uses his family farm in Llandrindod Wells to escape from the echo chamber of the game. Like George's home of

Ynys Môn, Llandrindod is a couple of hours north of the country's southern corridor of top-flight competition. So as a youngster Dan, too, had to make a journey south to pursue his playing career. Unlike George, however, his was taken gradually, the names of his junior and youth clubs picking out the stepping stones of his route: Llandrindod Wells, Builth Wells, Gwernyfed, Brecon, Newport Youth, Pontypool United and finally his current region, the Gwent Dragons. If he has a Friday match, then Dan takes the opportunity to reverse that trip south and will spend the weekend back on the farm. 'It's where I go to switch off,' he says, speaking as he often does through a gentle smile. 'I'll potter around on the quad, drive round the sheep in the fields. I come back the next week feeling that bit more refreshed.' He often does a bit of work too, helping out his father and brothers. Although as he admits, 'It's only the weekend jobs, so it's still a quiet time.'

Today it's Dan's family who've made the journey south instead. He saw his parents this morning at the Vale when they came to pick up their tickets. They always come and see his home games for the Dragons too, and always sit in the same part of the stand, between the twenty-two and the halfway line, so that, as Dan says, 'I always know where to look to find them.'

In a letter of advice to his son, Nicholas, the poet Ted Hughes once told him to always remember:

At every moment, behind the most efficient seeming adult exterior, the whole world of the person's
childhood is being carefully held like a glass of water
bulging above the brim. And in fact, that child is
the only real thing in them. It's their humanity,
their real individuality.

As the Wales team bus drives through the western
suburbs of Cardiff, it would be hard to imagine a more
masculine collection of men than those sitting inside. As
Dan Baugh once described them, 'They're clichéd macho
guys. That's why they play rugby. I mean, they're the
stereotype, right?' And yet what Hughes tells Nicholas
is perhaps more evident in these men than in most.
Whereas the majority of people have few visible ties to
the child behind them in their daily lives, this busload of
men are on their way to play the same game most of them
fell in love with as children. The twelve-year-old Warren,
still playing rugby barefoot in New Zealand; George on
the 'cabbage patch'; Smiler in the streets of the Rhondda;
James Hook, hoping as a five-year-old that his brother's
coach will let him play with the under-9s; Rhys Priestland
being taken to training by his grandfather and bought a
sausage in batter and chips as a reward. The childhood
games of these men have become their careers, the fundamentals remaining the same: the pitch, the ball, the
exhilaration and the team. All the squad on the bus have
been given licence to extend their childhoods, without

a break, into their adult lives. Jenks being coached by his uncles on Cae Fardre; Rob Howley's dad, calling him in from the roof of the kitchen extension, disturbing his imagined last-minute try at Cardiff Arms Park; Shaun sleeping with a rugby ball in his bedroom opposite a pitch. And Thumper, who after stepping in to protect his mother from his father had to leave his childhood home at sixteen and who has, ever since, found his families in a succession of rugby clubs and teams instead.

For all these men, as the bus carries them closer to the stadium and today's match, the child is not so much standing behind them as living within them, still breathing and feeling, just under their skin. Still playing.

A few seats down from where George is listening to dance tunes, the pace of the music providing a disjointed soundtrack to the slow progression of shops outside his window, Adam Jones and Ryan Jones are both texting their respective wives. For these men, approaching a possible third Grand Slam each, their years of experience mean coping with the kind of questions that face the younger players has become habitual. Becoming fathers has also given them a new perspective on their professional lives. As Ray Gravell once said on the birth of his own daughter, Manon, 'Rugby has been wonderful to me, but this is life.'

In one respect having children makes it harder for a player. Without any hesitation all the fathers on this bus cite being away from their families as the most difficult part of their job; missing first steps, birthdays, bank holidays. And yet the influence of their children also makes some elements of modern rugby easier. That crucial off switch that other players have to manufacture is there, an intrinsic part of your life. As Ryan says, 'I can't get psyched up for a game from Wednesday now because I've got two children, I've got other stuff on my plate.' For Adam, meanwhile, having a daughter, Isla, has given him something else to play for too. 'I want to make her proud,' he says. 'And she's another reason to keep going. I want her to see me play and to remember it.'

Adam has been discussing all week with his wife, Nicole, whether they should bring Isla to the match today. In the end they've decided she's too young (and, as Adam puts it, 'too wiggly') and this time she should stay at home in Merthyr instead. For the World Cup, however, when the squad were away for eight and a half weeks, she and her mother made the trip out to New Zealand to spend time with Adam. But then after the Samoa game they returned to Wales, and it would be weeks until Adam would see Isla again, which, as he says, 'nearly killed me'.

Ryan's three-year-old son, Jacob, is already in the stadium with his grandfather, Steve. There's no guarantee, however, he'll get to see his father play today. Having started for the injured Dan Lydiate in Dublin, Ryan has only started again for Wales once, against Scotland. He did, however, play and make an impact in both the other matches too, having been called off the bench to fill in at both number four and number eight. Today against France he's on the bench once more, although within a few hours, unknown to Ryan, Warren will approach him across the changing room as the team catch their breaths at half-time and ask him to step up again, this time at seven for an injured Sam Warburton.

With sixty-three caps and eight years playing for Wales, Ryan has begun to perceive his international career from an increasingly reflective distance. It is as if, in sensing an end to his Wales playing days, he's found himself thinking deeper on what his role as a player is *about*, as much as how it should be fulfilled. His advice to younger players, which Ryan gives in an easy, expansive manner, is to make sure they take time to step back, to consider what it is they've achieved and what they're experiencing. 'Otherwise', he says, with a slow Newport lilt, 'you just get caught up in it. It all feels like a natural progression. Without knowing it you've done five, six years, you've got fifty caps, and then it's over.'

A veteran of the various losses involved in being a winner at international rugby – of time, privacy and independence – in 2007 Ryan thought he'd lost the sport itself for good. When he woke in a hospital bed after a routine shoulder operation, the doctors told him he may never play again. The surgeon had removed a huge amount of damaged cartilage from his joint, in which he'd also made multiple micro-fractures to stimulate repair. It was a rare condition, and for a long time there was no clear path to recovery. The following months were dark for Ryan, and involved what he describes as 'a lot of turmoil'. It was, though, a turmoil that brought with it a positive resonance, the sudden disturbance in his career making Ryan a more nuanced player on and off the pitch, and more philosophical about the sport's rewards and sacrifices too.

On a day like today Ryan's reward, if he gets the chance to play and Wales win, will be to share that experience with his parents, wife and son. Much of what he achieves now Ryan sees in this light, as an opportunity to repay the investment his family have made in him from the very start. And in this respect he's far from alone on the bus. Some of today's players will have had to make their own way from the beginning of their careers. But others, like Ryan, will also have parents whose efforts over the years have contributed to them taking their seat today. Mothers and fathers who drove them across the country to matches, training and trials; who paid out for kit and supplements; who supported them financially and emotionally in the early days of their careers.

As the Wales bus continues its progress down Cowbridge Road, gathering a growing haul of applause, cheers and car horns in its wake, this familial investment is another entry on the manifest of past experience it carries with the squad. Along with the influence of coaches, the thousands of rehab sessions, the countless pitches and the years of training, these efforts of grandfathers, uncles and parents completes the bus's cargo of hinterland as, slowing at the junction with Cathedral Road, it drives on towards the River Taff, where from behind Castlebridge House the Millennium Stadium begins slipping into view.

The crowds have thickened now, down both sides of the road and along the central reservation too, their cheers and applause washing against the bus as it passes like a slow whale along the street. Up ahead the four motorcycles have been joined by four mounted policemen, their fluorescent jackets bobbing in a line as their horses trot at the vanguard of the procession.

For James Hook, listening to the Stereophonics' 'Is Yesterday, Tomorrow, Today?', this is the moment he used to dream of when he was younger. Like several of today's players, he was out there for the 2005 Grand Slam, in the crowd, watching the team bus drive past, wanting desperately to be a part of it. The squad on that bus had seemed so distant to him, unreachable, and yet within a year players such as Gethin, Adam and Ryan were his teammates, his elusive, gliding running style having won him a place in the national squad at the age of twenty-one. Warren's policy of trusting youth with selection means that as James looks out over the crowd, listening to Kelly Jones sing *Write down all the things that you'd like to be, write down all the places you'd like to see*, the chances are that somewhere among those thousands of faces a future teammate is looking back. A young player who in a year or two will be sitting where he is now, watching a crowd gravitate towards the bus, in which, somewhere, yet another future player for Wales will be watching and dreaming, *Is yesterday, tomorrow, today?*

As the bus moves onto the bridge, the players begin to remove their headphones, releasing a brief wave of music across the seats before leaving the vehicle in silence again. They want to hear as well as see what is happening. To hear the thousands of cheers, the wishes of good luck, the slow pulse of 'Waaales, Waaales, Waaales' that follows the bus as it crests the bridge and bears down upon the end of Westgate Street. As it does, the front windscreen fills with people, hundreds and thousands of them, most of them wearing red and all of them waving flags, scarves, hats at the bus and the players inside. Women blow kisses, men punch the air. A French supporter in a beret steps from the crowd and salutes with a baguette, held aloft like a triumphant spear.

Inside the bus it remains silent. Even those who have played in previous Grand Slams cannot believe what they are seeing. Adam Beard, who has worked with team GB at the Olympics, in Australian Rules football and in rugby league, has never seen anything like it before. He feels as if they are going to war, not a rugby game.

Warren, at the front of the bus, also looks out at the waiting crowds. Their smiles and their waves make it seem as if the match is already won. But it isn't, and if it still isn't at the end of the day, he knows he will be accountable. All of them will be accountable. He and the squad, as ever, will go to work with millions watching, and millions commenting on their performance. Because on match day everyone in Wales is a coach. The display of support still buoys Warren though, and he's hugely grateful for it too, knowing as he does that for the young squad behind him, what they are seeing at this moment is worth a hundred extra training sessions.

As a Kiwi, Warren is no stranger to obsessive rugby fans, and even the nature of Welsh support is familiar to him. Like Wales, New Zealand is a small country with a strongly working-class foundation to its rugby. Through the game's Maori associations there is also a sense of the sport representing and defending an ancient culture. But despite these aspects of familiarity Wales and the Welsh remain something of an enigma to Warren. With all the country's top-flight rugby crammed along the southern M4 corridor, to work in rugby in Wales is to work in a narrow fishbowl between Newport and Carmarthen. Warren has always felt that if he's honest with the fans, then they'll allow him the odd dip, a defeat here and there. But he also knows that, for some reason, the Welsh fans love the agony of their support as much as the ecstasy; that after the pleasure they seem to crave the pain. And that is why his biggest fear is still the thought that one day, as this bus drives into town, the crowd spread through the streets before them might turn. That one day, as they make this slow drive in towards the stadium, it might not be cheers that fill the air, but boos.

For now, though, as the bus makes its turn into Westgate Street, cheers are all Warren can hear, cheers and jubilation, as if the bus wasn't carrying a squad of young rugby players, but liberators rescuing the city after months of painful siege.

Matthew Rees looks out at the crowds below and knows that when his international days are done, this – this exact moment – is what he will miss.

In a similar vein, Ryan, too, wonders what he'll replace this with when he's no longer playing. This hit, like a drug, of playing for his country. The adrenalin as they run out of the tunnel. The noise and roar of the stadium's crowd crashing over them like a tidal wave. To have those thousands at your back as you bind with your teammates to sing the anthem. At thirty-one this already worries him, the life of aftermath on the other side of his retirement. 'I don't look forward to that wet Tuesday in Tesco's', he once said, looking out over a Captain's Run training session in London, 'when someone stops me and says, "Didn't you used to play for Wales?"'

*In the very temple of delight veiled melancholy has her sovereign shrine.* So said Keats. And so, in this moment of adoration and thrill, several of the older players, just as they feel their blood race at the sight and sound of it, also feel at the edge of their emotions the tinge of its passing. As the fear of defeat lies at the heart of victory, so the prospect of loss is at the heart of gain.

But all of this, now, is still not yet earned, not yet won. This support from the crowd is the cheering of hope and idolatry. Those other cheers, of celebration and thanks, are still waiting on the other side of eighty minutes, if they'll be allowed to exist at all.

Ken Owens, at the back of the bus, and the man for whom Matthew's torn calf muscle opened the door of selection, looks out of the rear window. Behind them the crowd that had been kept apart by the mounted police and the outriders is closing. 'Like the Red Sea,' Ken will say later. 'It was like the Red Sea, closing behind us.'

Matthew's injury, and then another to Wales's other veteran hooker, Huw Bennett, meant it was Ken who pulled on the Wales number-two shirt in the Twickenham changing room that February afternoon three weeks earlier. And it was Ken who read the commands on the tip sheet he found under his towel – 'ASSAULT THEIR ATTACK. BE RELENTLESS.'

Prior to that game Ken had only played one full eighty minutes of test rugby, against Namibia in the World Cup. He'd come on as a blood replacement against Scotland too, but then was off again before he knew it. In that changing room in Twickenham Ken was nervous, and found himself changed and ready well before the team warm-up. Unsure of what to do, he sat on his bench, his forearms on his thighs, his head bowed.

'Look up.'

The voice came from above him, soft and northern. Ken did what it said and saw Shaun standing over him.

'Lift your head,' Shaun said, advising, not commanding. 'You're a man now. Walk around with your chest out, like you own this place.'

Two hours later Wales, with Ken playing at hooker, had won the Triple Crown. In the stands Ken's parents, having watched their son win his third cap, remained in their seats to watch his sister, playing for Wales women, run out for her seventh.

As he looks out at the crowd closing behind the bus Ken sees a couple of his mates from back home in Carmarthen. He has been hanging around the local club there, Carmarthen Athletic, since he was seven, so it's well known in the town that he's playing today. In doing so, like all the team, he'll be representing them, Carmarthen, his home club, as well as Wales. When he was back in the town on Wednesday, the owner of the local cafe wouldn't take Ken's money for his slice of cake. 'You can pay for it', he told Ken, 'by winning that match on Saturday.'

The crowds deepen as the bus takes the corner into Westgate Street. Women wear daffodil hoods, men are draped in flags and nearly everyone is wearing some version of a Welsh rugby shirt. Along with the running applause and the general cheers, more pulses of 'Waaales, Waaales' continue to follow the bus as the police horses and motorcycles carve a path for it to make its final turn off the street and down the incline at Gate 4 into the stadium. As it does, Jonathan Davies, sitting halfway up on the left-hand side, sees, among the thousands of faces, his mother, waving and cheering with the rest of the crowd. The sight of her catches him unawares, and for a moment he feels his eyes welling up as the bus drives on down towards the stadium's underground entrance, past the four mounted policemen, past an ambulance and on into the darkness.

Almost immediately the sounds of the crowd fade behind them. Suddenly, after that brief exposure, the squad are isolated again. The bus enters carefully, as if boarding a ferry. Giant ventilation ducts run along the unpainted concrete walls; frames of folded growing lights are lined up along another. Making one last turn past Gwyn's security lodge, the bus finally comes to a halt outside the set of double doors leading into the changing rooms. Parked ahead of it, already here, is the blue bus of France.

Stewards in orange fluorescent jackets, ground staff and five members of the Royal Welsh Regiment, along with their regimental goat, William Windsor 25142301, look on in silence as the Welsh team disembark. Filing through the double doors, their headphones back on, the squad take the stairs up past the silver dragon and turn left towards the rooms that J.R., singing along to 'More Than a Woman', began preparing for them this morning.

From the moment the squad step off the bus, the machinery of the day steps up a gear. The next hour, with every minute accounted for, unfolds with a gathering momentum. The time of the kick-off is set at 2.45 p.m., and it will not move. At that moment the preparations will come to an end and the match will begin.

Once off the bus Thumper takes the team sheets to the broadcasters and checks through both countries' lists of players for any changes or errors. Then he travels in the VIP lift up to level five to drop in on the lunch in the President's Lounge. Checking in with Roger and Dennis, he tells them he's never seen as many people on the streets to welcome the bus as he did just now. Many of the guests, aware he's arrived with the squad, ask him how the boys are, how are they doing? Thumper nods tightly, telling them they're fine, good, calm.

While in the lounge Thumper makes time to see his wife, Kerry, who has been dining with the players' wives and girlfriends. Whether through arrangement or osmosis, Kerry performs a similar role with these women as Thumper performs with their husbands and boyfriends in the Vale, gently corralling them through the day's schedule, welcoming new arrivals and easing them into the match-day environment.

As Thumper talks with Kerry and the girls on level five,

four levels below Adam Beard, having checked the nutrition tables and written the warm-up timings on his hand, synchronises his watch with the match officials, then goes to see Lee, the head groundsman, to get his update on the hardness of the pitch. Lee will have already sent him a report this morning, but since then, with the roof now fixed and open, there's been a brief but heavy downpour. Based on his conversation with Lee, and having checked the boots France are wearing, Adam goes back into the changing rooms and advises J.R. on what boots and studs the team should use. This done, Adam's priority for the rest of the run-up to the match is to steal time.

Once Sam's huddle with the team is finished, Adam will lead the players through their warm-ups and pre-match drills, his aim being to keep them out on the field for as long as possible. He knows the shorter the gap between the end of the warm-up and the start of the match, the quicker will be the players' nerve conduction, the warmer their muscles and the higher their alertness. In previous matches, as Wales have continued warming up, opposing teams have often already returned to their changing rooms. Match officials will be telling Adam to finish so they can start the entertainment. Even Warren will be looking uncomfortable. But Adam knows how fine the margins are in international rugby, and how a split-second difference in the sharpness of one of his players could end up being the deciding factor between a win and a loss. So, like a chef trying to bring his recipe to the perfect temperature, Adam will steal time, keeping the players out on the pitch for as long as possible.

As the team are getting changed and having their strapping done by Carcass and Prav, and as Thumper goes to level five and Adam goes to Lee, Shaun, dressed in his team tracksuit, takes a stroll on the pitch. The heavy downpour, although brief, is concerning him. The French have requested for the roof to be open, and now, under the recent rain, the Millennium pitch is slippery.

On one of his arms Shaun has a tattoo of his younger brother, Billy-Joe, who was killed in a car crash in 2003, aged twenty. Like Shaun and their father, Billy-Joe was a rugby player. Before the accident he'd recently signed with their home club, Wigan. As Shaun walks on the Millennium Stadium pitch now, feeling the turf with his trainers, he looks up at the clearing sky through the open roof. 'Someone's going to slip today,' he thinks. 'And it's going to cost them a try. Please', he continues, addressing Billy-Joe directly now, 'just let it be one of them France buggers.'

## 2.38 p.m.

'Ten seconds, guys! Ten seconds for Wales!'

The suited event manager, holding one hand to the single earphone of his headset, calls down the corridor at the fifteen men in red standing in line along the wall. Moments earlier, accompanied by a sudden flurry of clapping and shouts from the substitutes, the Welsh team had emerged from their changing room, faces expressionless, their eyes focused beyond the cramped corridor in which they now stand. Lining up behind Matthew Rees, they hold that forward-looking gaze. Mike Phillips jumps twice on the spot. Jonathan Davies rocks from side to side. Jamie Roberts stands stock still. George North, further back, twitches his head in a couple of quick neck stretches. Alun Wyn Jones and several others push short, hard breaths through their mouths and nostrils, like penned bulls waiting for release. No one talks. Under their training tops, in memory of Mervyn Davies, the whole team wear black tape wrapped around the left sleeves of their shirts.

The French team are already on the field, binding in a tight circle against the noise of the stadium. The double doors to the tunnel are closed, but the sounds of the bowl, although deadened, are still audible. The waiting, silent squad can hear the pre-match music heightening to a crescendo, the bursts of giant flares firing at either end of the pitch, the announcer's excited voice echoing between the stands, stirring the capacity crowd louder and louder.

The event manager, touching two fingers to his headset, listens to an instruction. 'OK, Matthew,' he says. 'When you're ready.'

The double doors open and the noise is suddenly louder. With a deep breath Matthew Rees, who once pretended to be Neil Jenkins on the streets of the Rhondda, leads Wales out for his fiftieth cap. Walking at first, he breaks into a jog further down the tunnel. Behind him, Sam Warburton, holding the hand of Daisy, today's nine-year-old mascot, follows. And behind Sam come the rest of the team, stepping up and dropping through those double doors like a squad of Paras jumping from a plane.

In a clatter of studs the team stream down the tunnel, running past two Under Armour banners on either side: 'PROTECT THIS HOUSE'. Speeding up, they burst onto the pitch, fanning past Sam, who is crouching for a photo with Daisy. As the team sprint past him, all the flares erupt at once, shooting flames thirty, forty feet into the air and releasing a wash of petroleum fumes into the higher levels of the stands. At the same moment 75,000 people rise to their feet, delivering an imposing roar of a welcome as the familiar chant pulses through the stadium like a heartbeat:

'Waaales! Waaales! Waaales!'

And in the Three Kings in London, and in the Red

Lion in New York, and in Camp Bastion in Afghanistan, and in pubs and homes across Wales and the world millions of Welsh applaud and cheer at the same time, foisting their hopes and their ideas of a nation upon the twenty-two young men running out onto the pitch.

And none of it matters. And yet all of it matters. Because for players and spectators alike this isn't just about being alive, but feeling alive. This is where the known and the unknown meet. This is the arena, the coliseum. Where the present is electrified by its imminent transfiguration into the past. Where, as Philippe Saint-André said to an interviewer before the game, 'We do not just play against Wales, but against the whole country.'

As George runs onto the pitch he momentarily dips to brush his fingers through the whitewash of the touchline, rubbing them against his thumb as he sprints on into the middle of the field. Raising his hand to his face, he smells the scent. This, for George, is 'the final clunk in the cog', the moment when he becomes, for eighty minutes, a different George.

'Off the pitch I'm not that confident as a person,' he says. 'But once I smell that whitewash, once I cross that line I'm in a different zone. I find myself quite aggressive. Confident, but not arrogant, and generally quite mad at everyone on the other team. I don't know what it is, but it's like they've done something.'

George, feeling that switch of personality come upon him, gathers with the rest of the squad as they line up for the anthems, their arms across each other's shoulders. Next to them the French squad also come together, each player bringing with them their own hinterlands of past coaches, pitches, clubs and dreams. But as the two sides line up next to each other, they also bring their other histories to this moment. Not the histories of the players, but of the teams themselves. And as rugby histories go, they are as mirrored and balanced as the teams look now, spread either side of the halfway line.

| Wales | France |
|-------|--------|
| 15 Leigh Halfpenny | 15 Clément Poitrenaud |
| 14 Alex Cuthbert | 14 Wesley Fofana |
| 13 Jonathan Davies | 13 Aurélien Rougerie |
| 12 Jamie Roberts | 12 Florian Fritz |
| 11 George North | 11 Alexis Palisson |
| 10 Rhys Priestland | 10 Lionel Beauxis |
| 9 Mike Phillips | 9 Dimitri Yachvili |
| 8 Toby Faletau | 8 Imanol Harinordoquy |
| 7 Sam Warburton (c) | 7 Julien Bonnaire |
| 6 Dan Lydiate | 6 Thierry Dusautoir (c) |
| 5 Ian Evans | 5 Yoann Maestri |
| 4 Alun Wyn Jones | 4 Pascal Papé |
| 3 Adam Jones | 3 David Attoub |
| 2 Matthew Rees | 2 William Servat |
| 1 Gethin Jenkins | 1 Jean-Baptiste Poux |

| Replacements | Replacements |
|-------|--------|
| 16 Ken Owens | 16 Dimitri Szarzewski |
| 17 Paul James | 17 Vincent Debaty |
| 18 Luke Charteris | 18 Julien Pierre |
| 19 Ryan Jones | 19 Louis Picamoles |
| 20 Lloyd Williams | 20 Morgan Parra |
| 21 James Hook | 21 François Trinh-Duc |
| 22 Scott Williams | 22 Jean-Marcellin Buttin |

Wales have played France eighty-nine times. Over the course of those games they have won forty-three matches each. France have scored 1,304 points, Wales 1,305.

The more recent history, however, tells a harsher story for Wales. Of the last eight games against France they have lost seven. The last time they played this fixture, in Paris last year, Wales failed to score a single try.

'No one can take it away from you.' That's what Warren reminded the squad at their team meeting in the Vale this afternoon. 'When you win a Grand Slam, it's yours. No one can take it away from you.'

'We know we deserve to win.' And that's what Sam told them just minutes ago in the changing room. He used to stress about that team talk, used to write it down. But now he just says what he feels is right at the moment. Which, today, was this. 'We know we deserve to win, for us and the fans. We know how much work we've done.'

The media have been talking all day about the death of Mervyn Davies, another Welsh captain who twice led his side to Grand Slam victories over France. There has been talk of the team being spurred on by his death, being fuelled to play in his memory. But for the squad it's more simple and, in a way, more personal than that. Sam does mention Mervyn in his talk, and they all know a great player has passed on. But in the hardest moments of this match they'll be digging in for themselves and for each other; for the pain they've shared and the sacrifices they've made, and in answer to that banner in the Barn that asks, *How do you want to be remembered?*

For the next minute, however, it is Mervyn Davies and Jock Hobbs, the ex-All Black who also died recently, who are remembered as the full weight of a stadium's silence falls upon the pitch. For sixty seconds the two teams, the match officials and the 75,000 spectators all stand motionless as images of Merv and Jock come up on the stadium's big screens. After all the build-up, the bus journey into the centre, the superstitions of the changing room, Adam's stolen time, there is, before the violence of the match, this. A strange moment of peace, the loud voice of the stadium silenced.

When the minute ends, the anthems begin. The French who have travelled to Cardiff sing 'La Marseillaise' with energy, but when the opening lines of the Welsh anthem are sung – '*Mae hen wlad fy nhadau yn annwyl i mi*' ('The land of my fathers which is dear to me') – it's as if the volume control on the stadium has been turned up to eleven. For the players at the centre of the pitch it's an overwhelming experience. They've spent much of the last few hours trying to achieve a careful set of psychological balances: between aggression and discipline, emotion and focus, boldness and caution. And yet it's as if this anthem has been designed to ambush them. The words of Evan James of Pontypridd and the music of his son, James James, coming together just seconds before kick-off to lay an emotional minefield at their feet.

To keep himself together George finds one point in the stands as he sings, and keeps his eyes fixed upon it. Sam, although always 'singing out loud in my head', usually remains silent. But this time even he, his hand on Daisy's shoulder, sings, albeit in a subdued manner, as if, like in that letter by Ted Hughes, he's doing all he can not to spill something brimming at his edge. Adam Jones, his eyebrows Vaselined against the abrasion to come, sings with a concerned frown of care. Jamie Roberts, with his eyes shut. Alun Wyn Jones, meanwhile, uses the anthem to take him to the next stage of his day's preparations. With the sinews in his neck straining and the veins over his temples rising, Alun Wyn screams out the anthem's final lines, his eyes reddening and his head tipped back.

> *Tra môr yn fur i'r bur hoff bau,*
> *O bydded i'r hen iaith barhau.*
> [While seas secure the land so pure,
> O may the old language endure.]

The anthem ends in a torrent of applause, cheers and, as the players unbind, the breaking of the team's chain. Alun Wyn looks as if he's received terrible news, as if he wants to do someone harm in revenge.

Within seconds, as the field is cleared of banners, bands and choirs, the players are already preparing for kick-off. The French sprint and jog, swinging their arms, performing final stretches. Wales, however, have tipped to the far end of their territory, where the team engages in Adam's last few seconds of stolen time. In short, concentrated waves, they perform 'bag hits', running at Dan Baugh and the subs to smash into the tackle shields they hold before them. With each hit the shield-bearer is shunted a few feet back towards the dead-ball line, before reasserting their position for the next player and the next hit.

Behind them France are beginning to string out along the halfway line, so, turning from their final hits, the Welsh players also walk into position, scattering deeply through their half. Gethin Jenkins, the veteran prop, blows out a deep breath. Adam Jones calls instructions to the other forwards. Craig Joubert, the referee, raises his arm and blows his whistle. A fanfare sounds on the PA system and the crowd responds with a cheer as Yachvili, signalling to his teammates, drop-kicks the ball high and deep into Welsh territory.

The match has begun.

## o min.

Toby, who wears Mervyn's number-eight jersey today, and whose own father's playing days brought him from Tonga to Wales as a child, catches the ball and drops his shoulder to meet what it will bring. A sudden blue wave rolls him and his teammates backwards, breaking over them as they form a ruck and Toby lays the ball back. Mike clears, making the first of the six kicks to punctuate this opening minute of the match. The fifth is made by Rhys, searching behind the French line. Alex, with a sprinting style reminiscent of Michael Johnson, comes steaming after it, pressurising Poitrenaud to punt into touch and making Wales the winners of the first kicking exchange.

# 1 min.

The two packs come together to form the first set piece of the match, the forwards lining up in domino formation behind each other and next to their opposing numbers. The previous week the Welsh line-out seemed lacking, so for the past few days Rob McBryde has put in extra sessions working on their calls and moves. Unlike the scrum, the line-out is a set piece of moving parts: a thrower, two lifters, dummy runners and a jumper. If a call is to be successful, each of these parts must work off and with each other like the intimate mechanics of a watch. For Alun Wyn, lining up at the centre of the Welsh formation, it's as much about rhythm as memory. 'A good line-out', he says, 'will flow. It's more art than science.'

If that rhythm is right, then the line-out is also a brief pause button in a match, a slow-motion ballet with the jumper, which Alun Wyn is now, lifted to twice his height and suspended there for a second, held aloft by Adam and Gethin below him.

Catching the ball cleanly, Alun Wyn drops it to Mike at scrum-half, as if throwing it down from a first-floor window. At the same time as his rising, like the undoing of a combination lock both flankers, Sam and Dan, have popped out of the line. Taking a few paces back they both pause, each with one foot cocked, a mirror of each other, ready to spring forward.

It isn't them, though, who come onto the ball but Alex, charging in to take Mike's pass in his arms, clutching the ball to his chest as if cradling a child. Hitting the French defence, he sucks in two defenders before going to ground.

Mike digs in the bodies and spins the ball free, releasing a chained pattern of breaks, stoppages and passes that revolves through three phases before ending in another French clearance to touch.

Already Matthew, Sam and Jon Davies have all tested the French line, with Jon breaking through it, only to be dragged down by Fofana, clinging to his back like a cheetah jumping on its prey.

'But a line-out', Alun Wyn also says, 'is about possession quality, not just percentage.' As Matthew throws in, the ball is tapped down to Mike, who, having to scramble for it, is enveloped by French shirts. Adam stands in at scrum-half, but the slower ball has given the French time to prepare, so as Matthew receives his pass, he too is hit to the ground.

Just as there's a kinetic chain in each of the players' movements, so there is a chain of reaction through every period of play. Mike is back in position, pointing instructions, sending Toby back off a ruck. But the disrupted flow of that line-out is now in the rhythm of the Welsh game too. As Alun Wyn carries the ball into another phase he knocks it on and loses possession.

The French scrum-half, Yachvili, kicks downfield, and Craig Joubert announces, 'Advantage over.' Just as line-outs have rhythm, so do matches, and it is the referee, as much as the players, who conducts that rhythm. With this announcement Joubert is setting out his stall: in the interest of the flow of the match he'll be moving on from advantages quickly, trying to keep the flame of the game alight.

Leigh receives Yachvili's kick and returns a high, mortared ball back to the French. Yet another kick comes back, into touch in the Welsh half. This time it's Ianto, already over two metres tall, who rises even higher from the line-out to drop the ball to Mike, who spins it to Rhys, who puts yet another high, hanging kick into the air.

Last night Rhys went to the cinema with Jon, Mike and Jamie. They knew the roof of the stadium would be open today, and they'd seen the forecast for rain. Jon asked Rhys what was the highest number of kicks he'd ever made in a game. Rhys said he couldn't be sure – maybe forty? 'Well,' Jon said, 'I reckon you could be kicking all day tomorrow.'

And so far Jon's been proved right. The rhythm of the match is being set on the boot, not through the hands.

'Play in their half' – this is the Welsh policy. Kick and put them under pressure, no silly mistakes. It's a good policy for a match like this, in which France are trying to slow down the play. But sometimes for Rhys, wearing the iconic number ten on his back means that 'good' policy isn't always seen as the right policy by fans in Wales. Such is their expectation of a 'national' style that he's had complaints about him not 'playing in a Welsh way'. But the quietly spoken Rhys is a reader and a strategist of the game. Part of his role is to look for space on the field, to test their opponents' pressure points. And today, with a greasy pitch and a wet ball, this is how he'll be doing that – by skying kicks that send everyone's heads tilting back, and that give his backs time to chase and harry upfield.

Another Welsh knock-on sees the setting of the first scrum, the two packs kneeling and binding in preparation to knit together at the referee's command.

The etymology of the word 'scrum' has violence at its every root. Derived from 'scrimmage', itself a corruption of 'skirmish', its origins lie in the old High German '*skirmen*' – 'to protect, defend' – and the Middle English '*skirmysshen*' – 'to brandish a weapon'.

Where once the scrum was the most basic of territorial contests on a pitch, in the modern game it has, in Rob McBryde's words, 'become more of a hitting contest than a shoving contest'. Changes in the rules, and the relaxing of others such as feeding, mean the scrum, for all its base qualities of weight, power and aggression, is now also a subtle tactical arena of sleight of hand and one-upmanship. Where once a scrum was used to win the ball, they're now frequently used to win a free kick or penalty instead.

The two packs, loaded with the potential kinetic tension of their combined force, crouch and face each other. Gethin holds his free hand in a fist; Adam holds his open. The heads of the opposing props and hookers are inches apart, ready to mesh into the spaces between each other's necks, hitting shoulder against shoulder, driven together by the full weight of the packs behind them. The force of that collision is around 14.8 kilonewtons, 150 kilogrammes per 0.09 square metres, the equivalent of dropping a cow onto a person's shoulders from a metre's height and enough total force to uproot a small oak. For Adam's wife, Nicole, this is the hardest part of the game to watch, both because of that force and because she knows this is when Adam, at tight head, although unseen, has to perform the dark arts of the front row, when he has to dominate and pressurise his opposite number.

Craig Joubert, standing over the two packs, gives them their instructions.

'Crouch. Touch.'

The props flick their free hands forward to lightly tap the shoulder of their opposite number.

'Pause. Engage.'

Earlier this week, as they packed down against a scrummaging machine on a mist-covered Castle pitch at the

Vale, the Welsh forwards heard these exact instructions, spoken in the same rhythm by the same voice. Craig Joubert was not at that training session, but his voice was, emitted from an iPod dock held by one of Rhys Long's analysts crouching beside the pack. Such are the margins in modern rugby that a referee's intonation, the length of his pause, the rhythm of his speech can be enough to turn a game. Which is why all through that session in the mist the Welsh pack scrummaged with Joubert's voice in their ears, timing the wave of their drive, from Toby's first nudge to the impact of the front row, against that single repeated phrase, fuzzy but consistent in their ears.

And now, as the two packs engage at the Millennium Stadium, as they hit shoulders and sixteen pairs of legs brace and flex against the pitch, the timing laid into the muscle memories of the Welsh pays off. The scrum caves in and the French are penalised for early engagement.

Mike immediately goes searching for the ball, finds the mark, then taps and spins to Toby, who once again launches himself at the waiting French.

## 6 mins

Wales move through the phases, but with France barely committing to the rucks, their defensive wall remains strong. Gaining possession, Beauxis, their number ten, kicks upfield. Leigh returns with another high, lingering kick. Dan gathers the ball when it goes loose, the Welsh move finishing with Rhys grubber-kicking into space. A French drop-out from their twenty-two is returned with another high kick from Rhys, Jon's prediction of last night becoming more true with every unfolding minute of the game.

## 7 mins

When Rhys's kick lands, it's Welsh hands that collect it. Sam, dropping his shoulder, drives into the French line, with Alun Wyn lending his weight in support. But when he fails to keep that weight on his feet, France win a free kick, and then the line-out after it.

## 8 mins

With the echo of that iPod in their ears, the Welsh pack win another free kick from a scrum. This time Mike taps and goes himself, skirting round the still bound front row and piling into the French defenders.

Unlike his attack coach, Rob Howley, who had to fight for his position at scrum-half against those who thought he was too small, Mike had to fight for his against those who thought he was too big. Scrum-half is a position rich with association, those two words conjuring the image of a shorter, stocky man, terrier-like at the heels of the bigger forwards. A mini-general, commanding the game, who probes and darts at the gaps in an opponent's armour. For years scrum-halves have had their positions guessed by strangers in bars, simply by sizing them up in comparison to the other rugby players they know.

Until he was fourteen Mike fitted this idea. But then he grew, eventually reaching six foot three. Aware of his own size, it wasn't a Welsh scrum-half Mike admired when he was playing for Whitland and St Clears, but the tall South African, Joost van der Westhuizen. People telling him to change his position was just fuel to the fire, convincing Mike he had to prove them wrong and remain a scrum-half.

Mike displays a similar dogged quality now, as he

drives on into the French defence and is brought down, only to get to his feet and continue again, barging into the bulk of French lock Maestri.

There is a feral quality to Mike's play, and to Mike too, off the pitch. This has been mostly to Wales's benefit, providing Warren with a dangerous player big enough to be a third flanker, yet still possessed of that scrum-half guile and tenacity. But the modern game is about balance too, something Mike acknowledges as one of its biggest challenges. 'I've tried different stuff,' he says about his preparations for a game. 'To work myself up, or to chill myself down. But that's what makes rugby so hard. You have to be on the edge; you have to smash someone twice your body weight, then next minute you have to be composed, think about what's best for the team.'

The whistle blows. This time Mike got the balance wrong by half a second, not releasing the ball when he was brought down briefly. France are awarded a penalty, and the Welsh retreat to await the French kick for touch.

## 9 mins

The ball crosses the touchline inside the Welsh twenty-two. France, with one kick, are in their best position of the match so far. After winning the line-out they suddenly find their rhythm, rolling a maul towards the Welsh posts. Adam tackles Servat, bringing him to ground in a brief spiralling embrace.

Dan goes for a different technique on Harinordoquy, cutting him down below the knees and spinning him onto his back. But Gethin, who joined Dan in the tackle, doesn't release his man before going for the ball. Joubert blows his whistle and raises his arm, awarding a penalty to France in front of the Welsh posts.

The Welsh players line up under their posts in a strung-out echo of their anthem formation.

When Joe Lydon, the WRU's head of rugby, was playing for England under-18s, his coach told him before a fixture against Wales: 'Just remember, they're not defending their tryline, they're defending their border.'

That metaphorical border still remains unbreached, but from their position standing along their tryline the Welsh players have to watch, after all their effort, as Yachvili strikes the ball with his left foot and sends it clean between the uprights. A swelling cheer follows it over the crossbar.

Wales 0 – France 3.

From the restart Harinordoquy, the French number eight, gets under the ball and readies himself to carry it upfield. George, however, has pursued the kick and is there to haul him in, as if he's netting a struggling shark.

Leigh catches a French clearance just inside the Welsh half, but this time he attacks on foot, not with his boot. As he sprints towards the French, his smaller frame makes his limbs appear to move quicker than other players. Approaching the first French defenders, he slips on the wet pitch, but rebounds to spin through a tackle and drive on another couple of feet.

It was a Welsh full-back of the 1970s, J. P. R. Williams, who came to embody the attacking potential of the position. It was a Welshman, too, who first demonstrated that the last line of defence on a rugby pitch could also be the first line of attack.

Vivian Jenkins came from Bridgend. Having learnt his rugby at the same college in Llandovery as George, he won three Oxford Blues at centre before being selected for Wales at full-back in 1933. At the time the required qualities of the position were meant to be a safe pair of catching and tackling hands, with a good boot to kick for touch. But in 1934, during a match against Ireland in Swansea, Jenkins initiated an attack from his own twenty-five-yard line, finishing the play eighty-five yards later by collecting a pass from his winger to cross the Irish line. The purists were not impressed and it was suggested Jenkins had played beyond the boundaries of his position. It would be twenty-eight years before another full-back would score in the championship, in 1962.

As if in homage to Jenkins's inversion of his role, in the next Welsh attack Jamie, known for his crash ball and bulldozing of defences, delicately chips the ball past the French instead. Toby wins the line-out, but without clean possession, resulting in a slow ball eventually being birthed from a maul to Mike.

For the next minute the Welsh rhythms feed the game as they go through eight phases of play. But the French defence, varying their drift with different currents of opposition, sustain attacks from Alex, Ianto, Dan, Matthew in a repeated pattern of French blue extinguishing fire after Welsh fire. The last to attack is Leigh, once again turning out of a tackle like a spinning top, finally to be quashed under a deluge of French bodies.

As 75,000 spectators follow Leigh and the ball, the TV cameras tracking his route upfield, focusing the gaze of millions, several other pairs of eyes are looking elsewhere. Up in the stands in the coaching box Wales's attack coach, Rob Howley, is watching the spaces away from the contact area, following his players off the ball. 'My mantra about attack', he says, his sentences rising at their ends, 'is it isn't what you do with the ball, it's what you do without the ball. Your ability to get off the floor, to get to a support player. The ball needs a lifeline and someone to help, so the more bodies you have around it, the more successful you're going to be.'

In front of Howley, Rhys Long is looking at his computer screen. With six dedicated analysis cameras around the pitch, and another stitching images together to provide a floating, bird's-eye view, he's watching the same match several times at once. And he's also watching it on more than one level. Andy and Rod, his primary coders at pitch-side, are inputting the team's key performance indicators – line speed, timings, gain lines and clusters of activity. Another five analysts, meanwhile, are coding three players each as they watch the game remotely from their homes around the country. All of this information is coming into Rhys's computer live, so as he watches the players' movements on its split screen, he is also tracking the vital signs of the game; reading the rucks, breaks and kicks happening on the pitch in front of him as figures, maps and graphs. 'People always say to me,' Rhys's mother once said to him, '"Why doesn't Rhys ever smile on the TV?"' 'Because', Rhys explained to her, 'I'm in my office, working.'

Down on pitch-side Prav and Carcass are running a touchline each for the duration of the game, their eyes trailing three seconds behind the action. Like Prof. John sitting with the subs, they are watching for players left on the field after a collision or a ruck, observing their movements after a hit, ready to run onto the pitch if they see anything of concern. The subs, too, are watching the positions they might replace, ready to start warming up at the first sign of injury. Ken tracks the movements and tackles of Matthew; Lloyd Williams those of Mike.

In the south-eastern corner, meanwhile, Lee, the head groundsman, and his assistant Craig are watching the pitch itself. After their months of dedication, their weeks of coaxing the turf to grow, their long nights slow-walking its length, they are now observing its destruction. Making mental notes of the scars and gouges, they watch as scrums churn at their mown patterns, boots and studs send divots flying, and tackling players cut thin trails of mud in their wakes.

Yachvili is penalised for not rolling away and the game, having had its pulse quickened, pauses. Jenks and Adam bring on water for the players, and also messages, both men running communications from the coaches in the box.

The coaching team have noticed that the French are varying their use of a tail-gunner in the line-outs. All the Welsh models have been built on France's number seven being in the line, but he frequently isn't, positioning himself instead inside his number ten, ready to stop an attack from Jamie. Rhys Long discusses this with Rob McBryde. They hope the players have picked up on the change, but just in case they send a message on with Adam for the forwards: if Bonnaire is inside his number ten, then drive through the line-out itself instead.

As the team drink their water and Adam relays this message to the pack, Rhys Priestland lays the ball on the kicking tee for Wales's first opportunity to level the scores.

When Rhys was at Bristol University, Jenks would travel to the city specifically to help him practise his kicking. 'I was stunned I was getting that kind of treatment,' he says. 'Without Jenks most of us wouldn't be able to kick the way we do. And he always had time for me too, telling me, "Any issues, give me a ring," that kind of thing. He's a great bloke.'

That depth of history between the two men came into play during the England match, not in terms of Jenks's knowledge of Rhys's kicking, but in terms of his knowledge about his personality. Rhys was having a tough game, and for a while nothing was going his way. From up in the stands Warren discussed with Jenks at pitch-side over their radios if they should replace Rhys with the veteran outside-half, Stephen Jones. It was a crucial match and some would say there was more than enough reason. But they didn't. After the match Warren told the press conference he thought it was better for Rhys's development to learn on the pitch. Which is exactly what Jenks, having known Rhys since he was eighteen, had said at the time. 'He's not going to learn anything here sitting beside me,' Jenks told Warren over the radio.

So Rhys stayed on, his game improved and Wales won the Triple Crown. Those last few minutes on the pitch, though, were definitive for Rhys beyond his personal development. As with the end of the Ireland game, it was, he says, when he felt the *belief* of the team. In both matches 'we never panicked. It was quite strange being on the field. Myself, not being one of the senior players, if it's tight I've been used to people shouting, "We gotta do this, we gotta do that." But there was none of that. Warby would speak, Gethin too, just saying, "Don't panic, we'll get down there, no silly mistakes." I think it's because we'd trained so hard and we've got a lot of trust in each other as a squad.'

Rhys stands and steps back from the ball, still studying it, like a sculptor getting distance from their work. Turning his back on it, he walks further away before facing the posts once more. This time, as he looks at the ball he seems to have developed a more inward gaze. He takes a breath, licks his lips, blinks rapidly, before turning his focus to the posts. To his right Ianto is breathing heavily, his hands on his hips, sucking in the air he needs to recover.

Rhys looks at the posts as if they are a puzzle to be solved, as if he is trying to understand something about them. He glances at the ball one more time, then back at the posts. Straightening his shoulders, as if coming to attention, he returns his gaze to the ball again. Taking four steady steps towards it, he strikes it cleanly, with the sound of a cricket ball against a bat.

A sigh cascades from the stands as the ball hits the slender upright of the right-hand post. It rebounds to the French below and Yachvili clears it upfield and into touch.

Joubert, the conductor and referee, tells the forwards to 'get into line-outs quicker'. Both teams are trying to impose their own rhythms on the game: France slow; Wales fast. But Joubert is trying to ensure it flows too. This is, after all, entertainment as well as sport, business as well as a game.

Sam rises at the tail of the line-out to win clean ball for Mike.

Down the line Jon straightens the Welsh attack. The second-phase ball is passed to Leigh, running in from deep. He looks dangerous until a massive hit from Fofana picks him off both feet and knocks him to the ground. The crowd accompany the hit with a stadium-wide expression of empathetic pain.

'Your body almost shorts out,' is how Ryan explains being on the end of a hit like that. 'You have that white-flash moment, when you don't know if you've hurt yourself or not. You go through a checklist. Fingers? Toes? Arms? Legs? Everyone's carrying injuries, and you know you're only one bump away from being finished.'

Such are the impacts of the modern game that players' blood samples after an international have shown cortisol levels equivalent to being involved in a car crash at 30 mph.

Mike spins the ball from the breakdown of Leigh's tackle to Rhys, who punts it high into the French twenty-two.

Yachvili is there again, under the ball, but this time with the eighteen and a half stone of Ianto bearing down on him. Catching the ball with Ianto just metres away, Yachvili shouts, 'Mark!' and like a spell the power is taken from his opponent's run. Slowing before the French scrum-half, Ianto immediately turns his back and walks away from him.

And everywhere else on the field, too, the game is powered down by that single word, bringing each player's intention to a sudden halt. If the suspended jumper in the line-out is the game's pause button, then the call of 'Mark' is its reset switch.

Yachvili clears the ball into touch, the French defence having soaked up everything Wales can throw at them. And everyone knows, Welsh players and fans, that they still haven't tried to attack. Like Muhammad Ali's 'rope-a-dope', the French are letting the Welsh batter them. But are they just biding their time, or have they really lost the ability to counter against the giants of the Welsh backline?

Alex cuts into the French line at an angle, making more progress than most, breaking a tackle and tying up four defenders as he scrambles forward. Mike takes on the attack himself but gets caught in the cluster of a maul, the red and blue bodies suddenly collapsing like the opening of a strange flower.

'No boots!' calls Joubert.

## 18 mins

In the whole game so far Wales have made four tackles. France have made twenty-nine.

Wales have completed forty-one passes. France just ten.

Wales have had 75 per cent of the territory.

But France still lead 3–0.

A short move at the front of a French line-out unlocks a flurry of attack. Suddenly, they're off the ropes. The Welsh defence shifts into gear. A charging Servat is taken down by George. Both Sam and Dan chop at the French attackers with sliding sweeps at their ankles. The squad have developed this style with Shaun, and it is stunning in its effect. Throughout this championship Dan, particularly, has made it his trademark, bringing attackers down with such suddenness that they often have no opportunity to offload the ball. Dan, meanwhile, free of his opponent's fallen body, is often straight back on his feet, looking for the next threat to the line or jackal-ing at the breakdown for turnover ball. As Shaun understands, in modern rugby it's more often a case of defence being the best form of attack, rather than the other way round.

When the French are penalised at the breakdown, Rhys clears the ball far upfield into touch. As the team follow for the line-out, he removes his gumshield to give instructions to Adam to pass on to the forwards, and then to the backs lining up outside him. A reserved character off the pitch, when playing at ten both a maturity and a command settle upon Rhys as he attempts, as best he can, to marshal each period of play before it happens.

The two packs line up in formation, and Matthew, his right forearm bandaged in black, his right bicep patterned in tattoos, lifts the ball above his head, as if in sacrifice. In front of him, beyond the two lines of forwards, the stadium's West Stand rears up from the pitch, a tsunami of red, frozen in motion.

On either side of the line-out Mike and Yachvili rest their hands on their thighs, watching for the direction of the ball.

A series of calls are shouted from the Welsh forwards as, like the switching cups of a street conjurer, the dummy runners swap positions up and down the line. The ball goes long and Dan, lifted by Adam and Alun Wyn, takes it cleanly to drop it to Mike. Rhys chips through, but the ball is gathered by Palisson, who counter-attacks, breaking Jon's tackle, only to be cut down by Sam. This time, though, he manages to offload to Dusautoir. But, as ever, Dan is there, harvesting the Frenchman's legs from under him.

Which is when it happens.

With Dan is Alun Wyn, who on seeing the split second of a chance drives through to scramble the ball from Dusautoir and turn it over. The Welsh front row immediately recognise the opening too. Binding together, Adam, Matthew and Gethin dive in behind Alun Wyn to secure the Welsh position, the voice of the crowd driving them on. Their wave of a roar accompanies Dan as he moves from his tackle to the base of the breakdown and, with Sam shouting and pointing behind him, makes the pass to Rhys.

The ball is in Rhys's hands for less than a second before he passes it long, missing Ianto, to find Alex, a year on from his first fifteen-a-side game, picking up speed on the wing.

Ahead of him is Bonnaire, the French number seven, but as Alex side-steps off his right boot either the rain or Shaun's brother, Billy-Joe, comes into play. The flanker slips on the greasy turf and is left flailing as Alex surges on, outstripping Maestri, who also lunges at the winger's disappearing back. Stepping inside again, Alex passes a final defender, who also slips on the wet pitch. The crowd are on their feet now, screaming, willing him forward. The noise is so loud Alex can no longer hear his own breathing as he sprints over the French line and dives into the turf, sending tufts of grass spinning into the air before him. Immediately, he's back up on his feet, a single thought in his mind: 'Did I just do that?'

Confirmation that he did comes with the rest of the team and the subs rushing in to celebrate with him. As Dan Baugh hugs and picks him off his feet, the deafening applause and cheers of the crowd fill the stadium. Just two months ago Alex didn't know if he'd be in this team. Like the rest of the squad, he knew it would be a tight game. His job was 'to chase and clatter them, to keep looking for the ball'. Which he has done, and now, as he jogs back up the field, Jamie hugging him as he goes, Wales are leading France 5–3 and Alex's life, in a matter of seconds, has changed for ever.

As his teammates regroup behind the halfway line, Leigh converts Alex's try, and the scoreline, with eighteen minutes of the first half still remaining, stands at Wales 7 – France 3.

The match is far from won, but Alex's try is still a turning point, proof that Wales's method and the weight of those statistics can come true in the scoreline itself. The relief of the crowd is palpable. The muscles of the stands relax, as if the whole stadium has taken a collective deep breath. It isn't long, however, until they begin to tighten again. The expectation of a win crackles through the spectators. But the chill of possible defeat follows close on its heels.

For the rest of the half the earlier patterns of the match are repeated. The two sides continue to trade kicks; France's long and searching, Wales's high and testing. Wales, angled across the field for attack, continue to face up to the flat line of the French defence. By the twenty-eighth minute the number of Welsh tackles stands at only thirteen, while those made by France has risen to forty-six.

In the thirty-first minute the waves of Welsh pressure do, at least, offer up a penalty, which Leigh, with Jenks behind him, converts. The score is Wales 10 – France 3, and for the first time in the game Wales would not drop behind even if France scored and converted a try. But their opponents would draw level, which today, for fans and players alike, would not be enough.

In the coaching box Warren and Rob, in their number ones, and Shaun and Rob McBryde, in tracksuits, look on, frowning. In front of them Rhys Long and his computer screen continues to feed them analysis. In training Warren is wary of 'paralysis by analysis': of overloading a player with information before a match. But now, at the heart of the game, Rhys's statistics and measurements, as much as a side-step or a tackle, could win the day. Any messages the coaches have for the team they send via Jenks and Adam when they take on the water. But the time lag, and number of messages, has to be carefully managed. It's no good sending advice applicable to ten minutes ago and, as Rob says, 'As a player the last thing you want is a message every break. It undermines confidence, and then we wouldn't be doing our job.'

Down on the pitch, however, the Welsh team are translating their training to their playing in every phase of play. Rhys turns the big Harinordoquy with a judo throw of a tackle reminiscent of Dan's padded Red Room in the Barn; George, bravely exposing his ribcage, leaps to meet incoming balls as he has done hundreds of times on the Castle pitch, with Rob Howley throwing them higher and higher; the range of Gethin and Adam, the two Welsh props, is testament to Adam Beard's fitness regime, while all the players spider and scramble at the breakdown as they have done thousands of times against tackle bags in training.

In the thirty-seventh minute, however, an injury to a nerve in Sam's shoulder unleashes a furious French attack. As Matthew throws in for a line-out, Ianto, as if breaking from underwater, surges into the air but fails to get his hands to the ball. As it travels towards the line-out's tail, both Bonnaire and Sam jump to contest for it. As Sam stretches his left arm into the air, however, his right fails to rise. Bonnaire takes the ball and charges forward, triggering a French attack that runs the width of the field.

Sam, meanwhile, runs to the first forming ruck, cradling his inert right arm against his chest. He goes to make a tackle, and again his arm doesn't move. At the next break in play he looks up at the clock. Thirty-eight minutes. Two minutes until half-time, and he knows already, in the biggest game of his life and with the match still in the balance, that he will only play for those next two minutes, and then no more.

The half ends how it began, with a Welsh penalty, kicked by Leigh this time, once more hitting the right-hand French post and releasing yet another stadium-wide sigh of frustration.

Joubert blows his whistle and the teams, beneath a deluge of applause from the crowd, jog back to the players' tunnel, turning left and right at its end into their respective changing rooms.

On the pitch, teams of groundsmen, led by Craig and Lee, begin replacing divots and repairing, where they can, the damage done to their turf.

# Half-Time

From his position outside the VIP lift Geraint hears the squad returning to their changing room: the clatter of their studs in the corridor, the sound of heavy bodies sitting, of lungs working against chests.

The lift opposite him opens, and Warren and the other coaches exit. Geraint pulls at one of the doors behind him and lets them into the changing room, where, for a few minutes, he will hear them say nothing.

Warren likes to give the players time to catch their breath before he talks, to get their drinks and decompress from the crucible of the stadium in which they've just played for the last forty minutes. All the coaches have something to say, but they also have to remain calm. The temptation is to spill out their information immediately, to pass on what they've gleaned from their positions up in the stands behind Rhys Long's computer screen. But they don't. For the next few minutes it is each player's chance to salvage some time for themselves before they return to the pitch. For others it's also time with the medical staff. Dan is lying on one of the treatment beds, his eye bleeding, having his split nose stitched by Prof. John.

Sam, meanwhile, has already had it confirmed by Prav and the Prof. that he won't be taking the field again. When Warren learns this, he crosses to Ryan's stall in the substitutes area, set apart from the team, and asks him to step in at seven. Within minutes that private conversation is being broadcast on the BBC. Sam, Wales's captain, will not play the rest of the game. For a second time against France, and for a third time in this championship, injury has taken him from the field.

For Sam it's a massive personal blow. That boy who *refused to be denied* when running the streets of Whitchurch still wants to see this through, to make sure Wales put that World Cup semi-final, and this Grand Slam, to bed. But his arm remains motionless at his side, so passing the captaincy to Gethin he accepts, once again, that he'll have to sit this out and watch his team play France.

# The Second Half

When the Welsh team emerge from the tunnel, the crowd rise to their feet in welcome. The French are already on the field, bound in a tight circle, with their backs to their opponents' entry. Dan's stitched nose and cut eye are layered in Vaseline. Throughout the first half he repeatedly put his body on the line, cutting down the French attackers as if he were felling trees. By the end of this half, in which Dan will push himself to the point of breakdown, the farmer's boy from Llandrindnod Wells will be named as man of the match. By the end of this week he will be named as player of the tournament.

Five years ago, when he was nineteen and playing in his Heineken Cup debut for the Gwent Dragons, Dan broke his neck. In the wake of a tackle several players fell on him, snapping his head forward. He heard a crack and, after a few moments, as he lay motionless on the pitch in Perpignan, he started to lose the sensation in his arms and legs. 'I remember lying there,' he says, 'thinking, "Am I going to walk again?" It was pretty scary.'

The feeling in his limbs eventually returned, but an X-ray revealed a crushed disc, broken vertebrae and torn ligaments. Dan was told that although the surgeons didn't have to operate, if they didn't then any fall or knock could potentially paralyse him. He went for the operation, more for peace of mind than because he ever thought he'd play rugby again. For the next year, as he recovered, Dan worked back on the family farm. The 2008 Grand Slam was a dark time for him, and for much of the tournament he found it too painful to watch Wales play. He'd barely begun to fulfil his dream of playing for Wales, and yet for a while it looked as if his international career was already over.

A year later, though, and two years to the day after he'd broken his neck, Dan, at twenty-one, ran out at this stadium for Wales against Argentina. The night after the match he wore his Welsh cap throughout the post-match dinner. His mother, meanwhile, who with his father had made those ever-longer drives south, didn't stop crying until the Sunday after the match.

After some initial hesitancy in the collision area, Dan was soon back to his younger form, playing with absolute commitment. The psychological healing, though, took longer. When the Dragons played Perpignan two months ago, Dan was stretching his legs on the pitch when he saw the spot where he'd heard that crack in his neck five years earlier. 'I was quite emotional,' he says. 'And I had a lot of demons in my head before the match. I was screaming a lot. I just wanted to get through it. As soon as the final whistle went, I was, like, "Happy days."'

Craig Joubert blows his whistle and the second half begins, Rhys drop-kicking the ball above the waiting French pack. Dan and the rest of the Welsh forwards chase in pursuit, still forty minutes away from the final whistle of this match, from Thumper's wedding or funeral.

Wales open the half with an ongoing attack, Ryan entering the fray early, and Alex once again breaking the French line. But a different France seems to have emerged from the visitors' changing room. No longer satisfied with just slowing down Wales's game, they now put pace into their own, launching an attack down the left wing in response to another high kick from Leigh. In the final chase for the kicked-through ball Gethin proves again why he is the epitome of the modern prop, sprinting alongside Buttin to gather the ball on the bounce from an offside position. In doing so, while he saves Wales from a French try, he also gives France a penalty.

When Beauxis converts that penalty close to the Welsh posts, the scoreline narrows again, to Wales 10 – France 6. A single try by the French now, even without a conversion, will be enough to spoil the day for Wales. The numbers brought up on the stadium's big screens resonate through its atmosphere. Wales have failed to get away from France and now, with thirty-five minutes still to play, the French are chasing them. The ghost of Wales's own comebacks in this tournament begin to haunt the crowd.

For the next five minutes this new French team continue to play along the lines of their own 'national' style, probing at the Welsh backline with a series of attacks. For chess players, the French Defence is a playing model known for its solidity, but also for producing a cramped game. In a similar way, France today, though robust in defence, have strangled their game in being so. Now both they and the game open up. Where before the ball was traded in kicks, it's now traded in turnovers.

Dan continues to tackle mercilessly, tracking each of his targets for a few seconds before pouncing at their ankles to bring them down. But the effort is starting to show. When the game breaks, Dan remains on the ground on one knee for some time, his chest and back heaving with his laboured breaths.

Wales win a penalty fifty-two metres from the French posts, three metres further than the kick Leigh missed against France in the World Cup. Removing his skullcap, Leigh places the ball on the tee once more. As he does, a rendition of 'Hymns and Arias' begins to swell from the stands, serenading him as he steps back to study the posts like a mystery. Dropping his eyes to the ball, his inward gaze transports him back to Gorseinon once more.

And we were singing hymns and arias,
'Land of My Fathers', *'Ar Hyd y Nos'*.

Leigh strikes the ball clean and true, sending it end over end through the posts. This time he watches its trajectory and, when he knows it's good, allows himself a brief explosion of relief and pleasure, grabbing at the air and shouting in celebration. Wales 13 – France 6. Wales are by no means clear, but they are safer than before.

Yet again Wales have to defend from the restart against waves of French attack. Scott Williams, the saviour of Twickenham, briefly comes on as a blood replacement for Jon. Gethin, Toby and Dan all make more tackles. As the pack scrums down, Ryan crouching into Sam's position at seven, the statistics show the story of the half so far. Despite the score, it isn't pretty reading:

### Possession

| | |
|---|---|
| Wales – 40% | France – 60% |

### Territory

| | |
|---|---|
| Wales – 33% | France – 67% |

Wales choose a closer game, taking route one from rucks and mauls, picking and driving, picking and driving. The crowd rouse into 'Bread of Heaven', their voices willing the players forward. Inch by inch they chisel at the French defence, but France still aren't committing at the rucks, leaving their lines of blue solid on either side.

Alex eventually manages to break through, barging through two defenders in a row. But then, within minutes, the man who gave Wales their try gives France a penalty. Caught in a breakdown as the French attack, Alex is penalised for handling on the ground. Up in the box Warren and the coaches look on anxiously, expecting a French kick at goal to bring them back to within four points of Wales. But as Alex and the rest of the Welsh team drop back for the attempt, France surprise everyone with a kick to Buttin sprinting down the left wing. France want seven points, not three.

Buttin, however, is stopped short of the line by Dan. The attack continues, with Gethin and then Jamie putting in hits to slow its advance. The game pauses for a scrum, and for Jon to return from the blood bin. When the scrum finally hits, France are penalised for early engagement, the rhythm of Joubert's instructions catching them off-guard once more. After all Wales's earlier inch-work, nudging upfield, Rhys now, with a single kick, sends the ball deep into the French half and into touch.

The teams continue to trade attacks and kicks. George rises to meet a high ball. Leigh, Toby and Jamie all make ground with runs into the French line. When France return fire, Joubert's microphone picks up the sound of Dan's tackle on Buttin: a crunching thud of an impact, like a punchbag filled with wood swung hard against a wall.

When the play finally halts, players are on their knees all over the pitch. Gethin falls to his back and is treated by Carcass. Jenks, Adam and Prof. John bring on water. There is just over fifteen minutes left, enough for either Wales to secure their lead or for France to come from behind and deliver a defeat.

Taking advantage of this pause in play Wales replace a fifth of their team at once, bringing on Luke Charteris,

Ken Owens and Lloyd Williams, son of Brynmor Williams, who also played scrum-half for Wales. Although Lloyd's father never pushed him towards rugby and his old position, once he saw his son had fallen for the game he advised him to refine his passing by watching videos of Rob Jones, who'd played for Wales through the 1980s and 1990s. Lloyd followed his father's advice and, as he takes the field today, he brings with him more than a pinch of an older method of Welsh scrum-half play, not just in his passing, but also in a style more reliant on quick service and sniping, rather than Mike's more physical flanker-type play.

As Mike, Alun Wyn and Matthew touch hands with their replacements jogging onto the pitch in Cardiff, in New York the opera singer Bryn Terfel, watching in the Red Lion on Bleeker Street, gets to his feet and sings, the pub's wooden floorboards resonating with the depth of his voice. Encouraging the crowd to join him, Bryn leads the early-morning drinkers in a rendition of 'Bread of Heaven', as if even from there, three thousand miles across the ocean from Cardiff, their voices might rouse the team to victory.

Back in the stadium Wales continue to try and find a way through the French defence, while also fending off the increasing pace of their attacks. In the sixty-eighth minute, after a sustained push close to their own line, Wales are finally playing in the French half again. Up in the coaches box Thumper has joined Warren, Rob

Howley and Shaun. All three, no longer able to sit and watch, are on their feet. A faster, more urgent pulse of 'Waaales, Waaales, Waaales' washes through the stands as Ken drives through a tackle to make ground and Jamie, the ball held close to his chest, crashes forward.

Wales's efforts have brought the figures for the half back towards parity:

### Possession
Wales – 49%                    France – 51%
### Territory
Wales – 52%                    France – 48%

But then, with less than eight minutes of the game remaining, Wales are penalised in their own twenty-two for pulling down a scrum. France are awarded a penalty in front of the Welsh posts. From their own tryline Wales, looking battered and exhausted, watch Yachvili return France to within four points. Wales 13 – France 9.

Within a minute of Yachvili kicking that penalty, Wales are awarded one of their own, deep in French territory. As Alex bundled Trinh-Duc into touch, the French player deliberately threw the ball away. So now, with Joubert telling him, 'No need to rush, but no delay either,' Leigh once again finds himself placing the ball onto his kicking tee.

In the last pause in play Prof. John was treating Leigh for cramp. Just seconds ago he made a break through the French line, spinning through tackles until he was downed by Dusautoir. And now here he is with white-wash on his face, trying to slow his heavy breathing, once more lining up a penalty in the dying minutes of a crucial game against France.

For Leigh, his teammates and the crowd, memories of that final kick in the World Cup briefly resurface. Wales, only four points in the lead, are still vulnerable. They need him to kick this penalty.

Leigh himself is still nervous. The anxieties he shared with Jenks this morning have remained with him throughout the match. The kick is close to the posts, but also from a similar angle as the one which hit the upright earlier. But Leigh has a job to do, so as another rendition of 'Hymns and Arias' fades away with his steps backwards, he stops, rocks himself steady, eyes the ball, the posts, the ball again, then takes himself, as ever, back to that training pitch in Gorseinon.

The TV cameras pick out a woman in the crowd. As the other spectators around her stare towards the posts, she alone has turned her back on the kick. Bowing her head and with her chin against her knitted hands, she is praying. Her lips move as, down on the pitch, Leigh begins his slow advance upon the angled ball.

The sound of his strike is deep and true, the ball's trajectory clean. The linesmen's flags are raised and, as the stadium cheers, its thousands of voices as one, Wales go into the lead by seven points. Wales 16 – France 9.

The woman praying in her seat turns back to the bowl, looks at the score and slowly stands, unclasping her hands in thanks.

Leigh, replacing his skullcap, runs back into position, as France, still only a converted try away from a draw, restart.

For the last four minutes of the match the pulsing heart-beat of 'Waaales, Waaales, Waaales' ebbs and flows but never ceases. The stadium begins to rise to its feet in anticipation as Wales kick, run and drive up towards the French line. A line-out is lost but Ryan charges through. Lloyd's head is bandaged and Toby's shirt is ripped at the shoulder. Rhys tries for a drop goal, but it floats wide. The coaches in the box all look on, powerless, arms folded. France are slow to take their twenty-two drop-out, but when they do, Ken secures the ball. The forwards pick and drive, pick and drive, before briefly being driven back. Wales spin it wide, then drive on again. With thirty seconds left on the clock, 'Hymns and Arias' swells from the stands once more:

> And we were singing hymns and arias,
> 'Land of My Fathers', '*Ar Hyd y Nos*'.

With ten seconds left, the ball goes loose. Welsh and French players dive upon it, and with just five seconds to go Joubert blows his whistle to penalise France. Jamie and Gethin thrust their fists above their heads. Alex, out on the wing, jumps for joy. Dan collapses to the floor, close to tears. In the box Rob Howley punches the air at hip height, as Thumper applauds between Shaun and Warren, who both keep their hands locked under folded arms. Down on the pitch Ryan points up at the fans in the stands, as Rhys makes one last kick to send the ball spinning into touch. The clock goes red, and the crowd goes wild. Wales, as the Blims and the country had hoped, have won the Grand Slam.

Immediately, the Welsh players, all smiling, look younger, the relief of their victory rejuvenating them. Unlike the Grand Slams in 2005 and 2008, this one hadn't been about surprise, but about expectation. About coming true on a promise they'd shown and keeping a promise they'd made.

On the pitch, between their hugs with each other, the squad shake hands and pat the shoulders of the French players. Welsh flags give birth to dragons throughout the stadium, the crowd itself suddenly active, with fans jumping and applauding. Up in the stands members of that crowd reach across to shake Warren's hand, while Gerald Davies, a winner of three Grand Slams himself and a teammate of Mervyn Davies, wipes at his welling eyes. Down below him on the pitch three more players with three Grand Slams now to their names – Adam, Gethin and Ryan – come together to be photographed.

In the 1970s it was three backs who achieved that feat. Today, perhaps as a sign of how the game has changed, it is three forwards.

The players continue to celebrate as the presentation platforms are built between them and the victory banners are erected. From this moment on, the rest of the day and the night will be all about celebration. Later this evening the squad will attend a black-tie dinner at the Hilton, where the efforts of this match will begin to tell upon them. Dan will struggle through the after-dinner speeches, just wanting to go home and lie down on his bed. Alex's back will be giving him pain. Lloyd will have five stitches above his eye. Sam, still drinking Coke, will continue to cradle his arm, while for Leigh the release of those day-long nerves will prove just too much. After the meal, when the others are still drinking and making plans for where to go next, he will already be back in his hotel room, 'exhausted and ill as hell with all those emotions coming down on me'.

For now, though, the team will celebrate together, here on this pitch, with champagne sprays and victory laps, with medals, interviews and Status Quo's 'Rocking All Over the World' blasting from the stadium's speakers. Ryan's son, Jacob, and his father, Steve, join him, all three generations binding in a hug. Ryan cries a little, then, carrying his son around the field, points up at the stands towards his mother. Adam, seeing Ryan and Jacob, finds he needs a moment alone. He's overwhelmed by the win, but he's thinking of his own daughter Isla too, and how much he'd have liked her to be here. In the middle of all the thousands of faces he finds his wife in the crowd, and they share a private look of gratitude and promise.

By now Roger Lewis and the coaching staff are down on the pitch too. Dan Baugh is hugging anyone he can find, while Warren walks steadily through the squad and the still-falling ticker tape with his son Bryn beside him. Raising his hands, he applauds the crowd and occasionally allows himself the slightest of smiles. Roger, meanwhile, in an echo of that other walk they took together five years ago in Nantes, is strolling towards the centre of the pitch with Dai Pickering. Both are smiling broadly, everything they'd hoped that first walk would bring made manifest around them.

Once the squad finally leave the pitch they take their champagne bottles, medals and trophy back into the changing room, where J.R.'s order is, once again, undone by victory. Half undressed, they pose for photographs, as Gethin puts on the winning playlist, leaving Geraint, standing outside their changing-room door, in no doubt as to the result of the match. Breaking into song, the players celebrate not only their win, but also the hard work and the friendships that led them to it, their country which plays and supports like a club, and the feeling it gives them when they do – of being alive, now, and of being remembered.

Beyond the changing room the stadium itself is beginning to empty, the crowds spilling into a city already fevered with jubilation. At Gate 3, where 'Sweet Child o' Mine' rings out from the bars around Cardiff Athletic Club, everything seems transfigured by the win. In the dying light the boarded Inland Revenue building, the old Queen's Royal Garage, the County Club are all lent a more majestic air by the grandeur of the occasion. Even the strip lights of the NCP car park, burning magnesium white, seem to shine in tribute to what has just happened.

The tide of people who washed up this entranceway before the match are now flowing back down its incline, thousands of them ebbing from the stadium, taking their shared experience of the last eighty minutes into the city and across the country. Rising above them once more is the statue of Sir Tasker Watkins, his hands behind his back, looking out over the filling streets and alleys. On the plinth on which he stands his words are written on a plaque:

> I did what needed doing to help my colleagues and friends and saw more killing in 24 hours than is right for anybody.
>
> From that moment onwards I have tried to take a more caring view of my fellow human beings and that of course always included my opponents, whether it be at war, sport or just ordinary life.

Sir Tasker's words remain unread by the thousands streaming past him, the spirit of celebration keeping their heads up, not down. All their energies, which for the last two hours have so charged the stadium behind them, are now directed outwards. Like returning travellers rushing down a ship's gangway, they are eager to leave and tell of their adventures. For many this will be the sweetest moment of their country's victory: when what was so powerfully hoped for has been secured, and when the purity of that second when the clock turned red and the whistle was blown is still vibrant within them. Because already, even as they flow onto Westgate Street and St Mary's, it is fading. As the stadium empties and its crowds disperse, so too does the essence of that winning moment. As Yeats says, *Things fall apart, the centre cannot hold.* Within hours the stadium's crowd will be unravelled throughout the city, their celebrations often a perverted inversion of everything which brought about the source of their revelry. Bodies will lie in the streets, too much will be drunk, and the honour and *cymeriad* – character – of Wales's victory will be blurred under beer and kebab boxes.

But it will still be there, held by the stadium itself and in the collective memory of those who watched and those who played. Like Warren told the team before the match, 'You win a Grand Slam and it's yours. No one can take it away from you.' As the fans crowd at the bars and the players change into their black ties, this is true for both of them. However brief the lap of victory, however diffused in drink Wales's win may become tonight, however unread Sir Tasker's words, they are all still there, and will remain so, quietly resonant at the heart of this evening at the end of this day.

# AUSTRALIA

A winter sunlight washes amber over the Sydney coast-
line as the Wales bus pulls away from the lawns, cafes
and broad sands of Bronte Beach. Inside, the squad sit
in their familiar formation, their red hoodies and training tops pressing against the windows on either side. The
cuts and grazes of those who played in yesterday's test are
still stinging from the salt water of the beach's ocean pool.
The swim was brief but, together with the winter chill in
the air, enough to have left all of them with a sea tightness to their skin, an ocean cold lingering in the bone.
Which is exactly what Adam Beard wanted: a recovery
swim for their bodies; a cold dip to promote healing and
reduce swelling. But he also wanted it to be more than
that: to be a different kind of recovery session, one that
would help heal another kind of hurt. Which is why he
brought the squad here, to Bronte Beach, to swim in the
saltwater pool at its southern tip, to take in the rocky and
residential cliffs and to watch the surfers ride the riffs of
white-tipped breakers.

The bus reaches the top of an incline, pauses, then turns
right to drive on through the suburbs of Bondi, heading

north towards the harbour and the Intercontinental, the team's hotel. As the driver steers with one hand he puts on the tour playlist with his other, a collection of songs compiled from two choices by each player and member of staff. As the boys look out of their windows at the easy-going evening of a Sunday in Sydney, Eric Clapton's 'Wonderful Tonight' begins to play through the bus's speakers.

Yesterday, on a pitch marooned in the middle of an Australian Rules stadium in Melbourne, Wales lost their second test against Australia. It was an intense, tight game. As Robbie Deans, the Australia coach, said at the post-match press conference, 'We had to win the game three times, because we lost it twice.' Within four minutes of kick-off George had scored under the posts and Wales were already 7–0 up. The Welsh forwards dominated the Australian scrum in what Ken Owens called 'the old-fashioned way'. For the last ten minutes of the game Australia fought desperately against a Welsh lead of 23–22. At full time that scoreline remained unchanged. And yet Australia still won, with a penalty kicked at eighty minutes forty-three seconds by Michael Harris, a substitute who'd taken the field just minutes before.

Wales, after putting their all into the match, thought they'd finally won a southern scalp on southern soil. They thought, with the clock turned red, that they'd kept the final outcome of the three-test series alive; that perhaps, having beaten Australia at home for the first time in forty-three years, they might yet go on to be the first European team to win a southern-hemisphere test series. But they were wrong. When Wales were penalised for collapsing a maul in the final play of the game, Harris, on to replace Berrick Barnes, stretched his kicking leg, held his nerve and slotted the penalty to win the match. Australia 25 – Wales 23. It was the most painful of losses, summed up by Rob Howley in a single comment over breakfast this morning: 'It's a cruel sport.'

So this is the other hurt that Adam hoped the beach swim might help heal: the slow, enduring bruise of loss. The oppressive ache of defeat that has settled on the squad ever since Harris's kick and the final whistle that followed it. In the wake of that whistle Adam Jones stood in the middle of the pitch, looking both devastated and perplexed. Sam also stood motionless, his gumshield protruding from his mouth, his hands on his head. The team's belief was instantly transformed into disbelief. More than one of the players cried in the changing rooms afterwards. They knew they could beat Australia, but for a fourth time in nine months – at the World Cup play-offs, at home and now twice here – the eighty minutes of each match had proved them wrong. They'd come south to take the next step in their development, to once again make a little bit of history. But they'd faltered in that step, and now the three-test series was lost, the final match next Saturday an opportunity to salvage pride rather than go for the kill.

The bus drives on up Carrington Road, the squad quiet and distant, looking out of their windows in private thought. As they do, Eric Clapton sings over them:

> And then she asks me,
> 'Do I look alright?'
> And I say, 'Yes, you look wonderful tonight.'

Along the length of the bus the players silently begin to sing along with him. Mouthing the lyrics, they watch Sydney pass them by, their faces ghosted in the glass through which they look. No one talks. The bus drives on, the song plays, and the players sing,

> And then she asks me,
> 'Do you feel alright?'
> And I say, 'Yes, I feel wonderful tonight.'

\*

Just less than two weeks ago it had all seemed so possible. As the Welsh squad prepared for the first test in Brisbane, the same voltage of belief that had driven them through the Six Nations was still charging the touring party.

Wales had arrived in Australia in two stages. While one half of the squad flew on ahead to begin their preparations, the other half stayed on in Wales to play and beat the Barbarians. This meant that, as well as fielding the largest tour party ever – a total of thirty-four players

– Wales operated for their first week in Australia like a twin-engined airplane, with each engine running at different speeds. As half the squad recovered from jet lag and the Barbarians game, the other half trained. When this half went for recovery, the newly arrived players went for training.

Even without this added complication this tour is already a significant logistical challenge. J.R. has transported sixty-seven boxes of equipment from Cardiff. Thumper had already visited every hotel, training ground and stadium months before the squad arrived. In each hotel they occupy, the Wales camp takes over entire floors to recreate the components of their team room in the Vale. Within hours of arriving, the Wales staff will have utilised ballrooms and conference suites to set up a dining area, treatment room, laundry system, banks of laptops for analysis, leisure area with table tennis and a dart board, a press room and a briefing area complete with projection screen and whiteboards.

The injection of a touring party into the life of a hotel can make for a strangely integrated yet divided experience. As other guests travelled in the glass lifts of the Brisbane Hilton, their cars rising and falling in the tubular shafts like bubbles in spirit levels, they witnessed the hotel's interior suddenly infected with a rash of red. While the squad had a briefing session before their first test, a Sinatra impersonator warmed up in the lobby below them with a rendition of 'Moon River'. As an aircrew checked in at reception, the uniformed group was strangely echoed by a cluster of players having coffee, all wearing identical kit and compression tights. As holiday shoppers returned laden with branded bags, they were met by the sight of the Wales squad in shorts and flip-flops, setting out for a walk along the river.

When the hotel's Tongan night porter realised Toby Faletau was in the same building, he left him a note hoping, just for a moment, to draw him away from the squad's regime:

> Hi Taulupe Faletau,
> Just to say hello I am Vili Naupoto (relative from Tonga) working here at the hotel (night auditor) starting at 9.30pm.
>     If you have time it will be very appreciated just to say hello in person.
>     By the way my sons follow your career very closely and proud.
>     'Opa atu.
> Vilipau Naupoto

However daunting the logistics and the matches ahead, from the moment Wales landed in Australia their tour was fuelled by a positive sense of expectation and potential. Much of this was imposed by the Australian and Welsh media, but in the two weeks before the Melbourne test it was also genuinely felt at the heart of the touring party itself. As Shaun Edwards said at a press conference, 'Usually at this time of year the boys would be in bits. But they're not, they're in good shape.' At the first full-squad training session at Ballymore, in the north of Brisbane, the tantalising possibility of winning this series, of beating Australia on their home ground was palpable in the atmosphere. The stadium and pitch is used by the Queensland Reds as a training facility, so Wales trained at night, under floodlights, when they could have the ground to themselves.

As the squad warmed up with Adam Beard in the middle of the field, one of Rhys Long's analysts, Rod, set up his filming and monitoring equipment high at the back of a grandstand. Thumper, meanwhile, walked into the shadows beyond the floodlights' glare to check for less welcome cameras spying on the session. A photograph taken of Wales training earlier in the week had already appeared in one of the papers. 'The buggers always try it on,' Thumper said, before heading off, his satchel across his shoulder, to walk the bounds of the pitch. Accompanied by the metallic tang in the winter air and the croaking of cane toads from the marshes at the ground's edge, he walked beyond the floodlight's island of light and on into the darkness. As he got further from the squad, they became increasingly diminished under the floodlights' glare, until they were no more than a red seam between the green of the pitch and the black night sky; a thin red line moving as one between the posts.

The connotations of that phrase – *thin red line* – are, perhaps, suitable for a rugby squad on tour. Wales are isolated out here; on unfamiliar territory, without their usual support networks back home. As such, in relation to their alienation, their unity is further emphasised. Most of the squad have purchased pocket Wi-Fi devices, and all of them tweet, Facebook and email regularly. But there's still a sense that all they have out here is each other. That on these pitches of southern soil on the other side of the world the *idea* of a team is somehow stronger; that like an invasion force the further from home they travel, the more they embody and represent the country in whose name they have arrived.

There is, though, also something of the Trojan Horse about the character of a touring party's invasion. Everywhere Wales have been they have been welcomed. The Australian Rugby Union have hosted dinners and events for Roger and the other members of the WRU travelling with the squad. The local media have attended the press conferences and have, on the whole, been generous. The players are stopped for autographs and photos. And yet they are all here with a single intention: to cause damage to the national psyche of their hosts. To beat a country which prides itself on sporting prowess on its own doorstep.

At the end of the squad's training in Ballymore the three kickers on the tour – Leigh Halfpenny, Rhys Priestland

and James Hook – stayed behind to practise. After the explosive defence and attack drills of the previous hour their session was, by comparison, a meditative caesura of calm focus. With just the three of them and Jenks on the pitch, the ground suddenly seemed larger under the floodlights; expansive and inviting. To a regular punch and thud of balls struck and landing, all three of them, working independently, once again went through their routines for place-kicking at goal.

The kickers are the snipers of a team; the individuals who, if on form, can single-handedly destroy an opposition, chipping away at their scoreline with penalties, drop goals and conversions. Even when not scoring points, a kicker who's found the perfect weight of punt against that day's wind and weather, who can read the spaces on the field will cruelly punish the other team. However hard-fought gaining their territory may have been, a series of kicks at the right time into the right space will have them repeatedly turning and sprinting back down the field, eating up the metres of their endeavour as they do.

Just as a sniper in a military company will stand apart, will train their eye alone, so the kickers in a rugby squad need their solitary moments, quiet codas at the end of a session in which to hone the destructive quality of their boot.

As the Wales kickers practise at Ballymore, they reveal, with each kick, the attributes of their styles, still visible within the architecture of Jenks's teaching.

As Leigh settles himself after stepping back from the ball, he stutters the toe of each boot into the turf, giving his right toe one more tap than his left.

For James, at the same moment, it's a downward brush of the right toe across the left calf.

Rhys, however, prefers to keep still, planting the toe of his kicking boot behind him like a horse resting a hoof.

The ball in front of Leigh is sharply angled on the tee towards the posts. James's is more upright, while Rhys's is the most upright of all.

Leigh's first slow steps towards the ball are like that of a cat stalking its prey. As he begins to tip forward he flicks his eyes to the posts once more, as if looking up at the call of his name.

For James, it's as if he's descending the stairs, lowering himself with each step, pressing his aquiline features closer to the ball.

For Rhys, his first steps are like taking a stroll.

And then all three of them speed up. All three, in a sudden explosive moment, take their final strides quickly, plant their left foot beside the ball and strike through it with their right, their bodies scissoring with the effort.

For a split second, as the ball flies from the tee, they are also in the air, suspended, with neither boot touching the turf.

When they make contact again, for all three it is with their kicking boot, snapped to the ground like the closing of a predator's jaw.

And then, with Jenks watching and commenting, a ball under each arm as he patrols the field, they do it again. And again. And again. With the cane toads croaking in the darkness and the temperature falling, Leigh, James and Rhys kick at those posts from their positions on the pitch, unsatisfied with anything other than the ball bisecting them as cleanly as possible. And then they start again, changing their positions, each man throwing his tee ahead of him like a gambling chip thrown to a casino's baize.

Three days later the air of expectation felt at that training session in Ballymore was still tangible as Queensland rugby fans streamed into the Suncorp Stadium in Brisbane for an 8 p.m. kick-off. Welsh supporters took their seats among the Australian crowd with memories of the Grand Slam still fresh in their minds, as if they held a secret of which their hosts were ignorant. Up in the commentary box Gwyn Jones, whose broken neck had brought Dan Baugh to Wales and Rob Howley into his captaincy, was also hoping his debut match as S4C's 'first voice' would be a historic Welsh win down under.

The day before Gwyn had dropped in on the kickers' practice, the shiver of his injury still evident in his gait as he'd walked alongside the pitch watching their form. A shrewd commentator on the game, Gwyn knows this squad well, and what he saw at that practice session bolstered his hopes for their success. The kickers and coaches all broadcasted the same calm steadiness that had seen them through their Six Nations campaign. Australia, meanwhile, were still fending off home criticism after their 6–9 loss to Scotland in hurricane conditions at Newcastle just four days earlier. So as he settled his headphones over his ears, with swallows and moths flying through the beams of the floodlights, Gwyn was confident about the Welsh potential in the match ahead. He was, however, also aware of their weaknesses.

This would be the first match Rhys had played at ten without the injured Jamie Roberts on his shoulder. The big centre had always been his fall-back position on a flat option throughout the Six Nations, so it remained to be seen what he'd do without him there. Similarly, the two centres who'd been paired in his absence, Jonathan Davies and Ashley Beck, hadn't played top-flight rugby for two months. Despite the Scottish defeat, Australia were still number two in the world, and would be eager to answer their critics in the media. Wales would have to slow Australia down. If they didn't, they'd be sucked into a fast game, and that alone could be enough to spell defeat.

That night after the match the treatment room of the Wales camp at the Brisbane Hilton resembled a casualty clearing station. Several players lay prone on the treatment beds, while others were on the floor, propped up against the wall. Scott Williams was still in hospital having his mouth stitched after a clash of heads with

Tatafu Polota-Nau; George North was receiving treatment for a dead leg; and Leigh was having a large piece of gauze strapped to his back. For many of the Welsh players the match had been the fastest they'd ever experienced. Intense, and with a high ball-in-play time, it had also been relentless. Luke Charteris said he'd wanted 'the pause button pressed' when it was still the first half. Unlike their opponents, who'd just been through the Tri-Nations tournament, many of the Welsh players had had a break from top-flight rugby, and it had showed. At the end of the match Wales looked exhausted. They were also, despite a comeback in the second half, soundly beaten, losing 27–19 to their hosts. They'd lost, and they'd deserved to.

But this second defeat they'd just suffered in Melbourne last night was different. Against all the odds and the historical trend of an opening match setting the tone for a series, Wales had come out fighting and, for much of the game, had been on top. So this time the defeat didn't feel like a loss, but more like a win that had been stolen from them. And that's why, as the team bus begins to drop past the botanical gardens and towards their hotel, the beaked dome of the Opera House cresting above the trees beyond, the atmosphere inside is still so leaden. Despite the swim in the ocean pool, and almost twenty-four hours since the final whistle, the hurt is still there, inlaid throughout the squad: in their expressions, their postures and in the heaviness of their tread as they disembark from the bus and file into the lobby of the Intercontinental.

Two months before Wales left for this tour Warren Gatland fell ten feet while cleaning windows at his Waihi beach house in New Zealand. He landed on concrete, shattering his right heel bone and fracturing his left. There was no way he would recover in time, so for once it was a coach, not a player, who was ruled out of a tour through injury. Rob Howley, Warren's assistant coach, stepped up to take over the squad. Although Rob has remained in close contact with Warren since, and despite him working with Wales since 2007, this was a seismic shift in his role. The final decisions – in selection, policy and training – were now his. With the change of a single word in his job title – from assistant coach to caretaker coach – his own words instantly gathered more weight, and with that weight, consequence.

Today, in the wake of the Melbourne defeat, Rob is clear about what the squad should do. They will stop. For two days they'll pause the tour's relentless routine and briefly disperse. The players need space and perspective to process what happened last night in Melbourne. A loss like that leaves a residue of grief in a squad, an emotion which must be respected and given time to run its course. On Wednesday they will regroup, assess what went wrong and plan their strategy for the final match of the series. But for now, for the next two days, they will no longer have to obey the kit instructions on Thumper's day sheets, the training will pause and all the players, within the limits of their alcohol ban, will be free to do what they want.

The break is welcomed by the squad. They have only been in Australia for two weeks, but already the twice-recycled tour routine of train, play, travel is starting to feel attritional. Including a midweek game against the ACT Brumbies in Canberra they've now played three matches, passing endlessly from plane to bus to hotel to bus to training pitch to gym to hotel to bus to plane. Predictability and boredom have become daily challenges. Shaun has travelled with a biography of Vladimir Putin under his arm, Rob McBryde with Emma Donoghue's novel *Room*, while Roger Lewis has been reading Bruce Chatwin's hymn to the outback, *The Songlines*. But for most of the squad, apart from their online lives and computer games, there has been little distraction from the focus of the tour: rugby. The free time they've had so far has been brief and isolated, leaving many of the players looking more disorientated than relaxed. Dividing into smaller groups they've gone shopping or hung around in the hotels drinking coffee, their explosive bodies restless in the muzak of the gilded lobbies. At these times, out of kit, their own clothes bestow their ages upon them once more. Along with those clothes and that age some have also adopted a surly uncertainty, a vulnerability even. 'You have to remember,' Ryan Jones says one day, 'most of us are just ordinary Welsh boys who just happen to have been good at rugby. Then, suddenly, you're playing for Wales, travelling in business class all over the world.'

Ryan himself, frustrated by years of 'travelling everywhere but going nowhere', encourages some of the other players to use one of their free days to join him on a walk across the top of Sydney Harbour Bridge. Ianto, Alun Wyn, Adam Jones, Gareth Delve and the squad's sports scientist Ryan Chambers sign up. The following morning the group put on the BridgeClimb jumpsuits and walk through the girders and ladders of the bridge to crest its highest point on a bright afternoon. Several Australians recognise them as they climb. Many commiserate with them for the loss in Melbourne, and more than one even says they hope Wales win the final test on Saturday. 'You was robbed, boys,' one man shouts through the wind as he descends the opposite arc. When they get to the bottom, the woman running the BridgeClimb office turns out to be from Llangynidr. She gives them all an extra photo of their climb, telling them, 'Just beat the Aussies on Saturday.'

Other members of the squad use the time off to visit Bondi and Manley beaches, which is where Thumper heads too, going snorkelling in the shallows. In the evening nearly all the squad go to a rugby-league match, also in Manley, and most take up the invitation to attend a Lady Gaga concert in her *Born This Way* tour. On the bus on the way to the gig Gethin plays dance tunes from the playlist, while Roger is on the phone to Wales, setting up TV deals and discussing court cases. At the gig itself the squad enter backstage and are impressed, if not animated, by Gaga's show, tapping their feet and nodding their heads as they stoically remain in their seats while the rest of the arena stands up and dances. The following night a smaller party – Shaun, Ken, Roger and WRU press officer Simon Rimmer – go to a performance of Dylan Thomas's *Under Milk Wood* in the Sydney opera house. The next morning over breakfast Ken tells Dan, Sam and others about the show, describing the set, music and how the actress playing Mae-Rose Cottage had drawn red lipstick round her nipples.

When the squad come together in the team room on Wednesday they are reanimated, fresher and ready to start again. The first briefing of the day will be an assessment and analysis of the match they lost in Melbourne. The atmosphere is akin to a sixth-form common room on exam results day. Music plays – Stereophonics' 'Local Boy in the Photograph' and Tracy Chapman's 'Fast Car', to which Dan silently sings as he reviews footage of the game's line-outs on a laptop. Then, without warning, and with that osmosis-like communication of the day sheet, the squad gather in the chairs assembled before the projection screen linked up to Rhys Long's laptop. As the players wait for the briefing to begin, Rhys's baby daughter, gigantic on his desktop wallpaper, stares down at the assembled squad from the screen above.

Shaun opens proceedings with a review of their defence. Speaking quietly he directs his comments at individuals. Those singled out nod in understanding and agreement with their own shortfalls. Decisions made instinctively at high speed, mid-game, are reviewed, slowed down on the screen and meticulously dissected. 'We're *assuming*', Shaun tells the players by way of rounding off, 'the tackles will be made. Don't.'

Warren has been with the tour since Melbourne, but Rob Howley is the head coach now, so, as he has since he arrived, Warren stays quiet as Rob steps up to speak.

'We've had two days to process last Saturday's defeat,' he tells the squad. 'We've seen the sights of Sydney, now it's time to go to work. We've jumped to fourth in the world rankings, and we should be proud of that. But now we need to stay there. We all know the game was ours on Saturday. We lost it because of *individual* decisions made by players *on their own*. As the coaches we can set the policies, but you have to play *within* these policies.'

Rob asks Sam if he has any words. Sam shakes his head, leaving it to Jenks to address the squad and announce the team. An almost imperceptible tremor of attention passes through the squad. One of Wales's greatest strengths this last year has been the competition for places. Every member, including the senior players, has to compete for his shirt. From this announcement onwards a subtle division will evolve through the following days' preparations, between those chosen to play and be on the bench, and those not. Roles will be allocated accordingly in training, with increased attention for those selected from the medical and conditioning staff. The team, within the squad, will quietly define itself.

Jenks reads through the team sheet in his usual quick oscillating rhythms, matter-of-fact, down-to-earth. There is just one change – the hooker Ken Owens on the bench instead of Richard Hibbard. It was Hibbard who was penalised for collapsing the maul at the end of the match in Melbourne. Nothing else need be said. His punishment is in his omission; in not, on Saturday, being a part of Wales.

Before the squad disband for training, Warren, for the first time on this tour, stands from his chair and, leaning on his crutch, steps forward to address the players. He tells them just two things. Firstly, if they are to win, then they have to win 'the battle of halfway' first. They have to make sure they play their rugby in the Australian half, not theirs. 'It is', he tells them, 'like a game of chess, a waiting game.' In the first test, he points out, there were just six line breaks made by each side. In the second there were only two. The opportunities are few, he reminds them, so when they happen, make sure they happen 'between the halfway line and *their* twenty-two, not ours.'

Warren's second point is more incentive than advice. 'There's a big tour next year,' he says dryly, referring to the Lions tour of Australia, for which he's tipped to be the coach. 'So it's time to put down a marker.'

The training after the team meeting, held between the 1930s stands of the North Sydney Oval, is rigorous, energetic and charged with enthusiasm. The squad look fresher for their time off. Having accepted they've lost the series, they're now hungry for a win. A seaplane flies through the clear sky overhead and a flock of ibises stalk the ground as the Welsh players, harried by Rob and Jenks, hammer into tackle bags, practise miss passes and run through their moves. Warren, sitting in a plastic garden chair surrounded by scattered training equipment, looks on, one hand to his chin, thoughtful. Thumper strolls up beside him. Holding his phone, his glasses are still perched on the end of his nose after sending a text. 'There's some bewts,' he says, nodding at James Hook and Mike Phillips. 'Now they're sweating.'

'Remember what this feels like.'

This is what Rob Howley tells the Welsh team as they sit in their changing room at the Allianz Stadium having lost, once again, to Australia, 20–19.

In the second half Wales twice took the lead, only to lose it again in the seventy-fifth minute, when Berrick Barnes kicked a penalty.

Ryan, the only Welsh try-scorer, has broken his nose.

The oil-spill colours of the bruising are already spreading under his eyes.

Throwing his body into a tackle, Sam received a knock to the head. In the twenty-fifth minute he was being sick on the pitch. In the twenty-eighth he once again had to leave the field and watch his team play on without him.

Leigh kicked fourteen of Wales's points. One of his penalties, though, hit the upright of the post. It was his first miss in sixteen match kicks at goal.

The game itself was tight and riddled with penalties. Twenty-four in the whole match, with many offside calls made by the linesmen.

At half-time, just three points adrift of Australia, with the score at 12–9, the other figures of the match were still stacked in Wales's favour:

**Possession:** 56%
**Territory:** 59%

More statistics, however, illustrated how closely the teams were matched:

**Missed tackles**

Wales – 10                    Australia – 10

**Line breaks**

Wales – 1                    Australia – 1

But as Wales sit in their changing room, their heads bowed, none of these numbers matter to the squad. The only ones that do are those which tell the result of the series: three–nil to Australia.

The Welsh squad embarked on this tour in the hope of winning either the series itself or at least a match. But as the lines and logos of the Allianz pitch are hosed away by the stadium staff, as the spectators walk back to their cars past creeper-hung trees, the squad know they have done neither. The word they most wanted to avoid is now theirs to own: whitewash. This is what the tour has been, and none of them, players or coaches, will hide from the fact, however much they wish it wasn't true.

At noon the next day the whole squad are having lunch at a seafood restaurant beside the pavilion on Bondi Beach. This afternoon they will fly home. After landing at Heathrow, the team bus will take them to Cardiff, where, after their three weeks together, they will disperse. Last night, however, presented with the prospect of their first long break from rugby and rehab for over eighteen months, the Wales squad celebrated and commiserated together. Pooling the tour's fine money, they bought crates of beer and began the evening drinking and singing at the hotel. Then, boarding the same coach that had taken them to and from the last test match, they went out into the city.

The teetotallers in the squad remained as such, but

many of those who'd been on alcohol bans for months on end finally got to break their fast. This morning several of the squad still haven't been to bed. At this lunch on Bondi Beach, the drinks are still being ordered. When other Sunday diners enter the restaurant, they're met by the sight of over forty large men in red occupying its entire central area. Some take photos, others frown for a moment before a friend or partner reminds them, 'Wasn't there a rugby game on or something?'

At one table at the far end of the room James Hook is holding court. Standing from his chair he points towards Ianto, sitting at another table. Having got married in Greece during the first week of the tour, Ianto had to forego his honeymoon to join the squad here in Australia. When he'd arrived in Brisbane he was fined twice, once for joining the tour late and again for 'being a shit husband'.

Because the rest of the squad missed Ianto's wedding, James thinks they should restage the nuptial dinner here and now, in the restaurant at Bondi. Pointing at other members of the squad he apportions their roles. 'You can be father of the bride,' he says, pointing at Ken. Then, pointing to Adam Jones, sitting beside Ianto, 'Bomb's the bride. I'll be best man!'

One by one the other players oblige, standing and delivering short speeches, thanking the bridesmaids and praising the qualities, or not, of the groom. The coaching staff look on from further up the dining room as a bizarre version of Ianto's wedding unfolds before an all-male congregation in red.

Despite the laughter and the drink, yesterday's defeat is still here, its resonance carried into the restaurant with the squad. Each of the players bears it individually too, both in the stud marks and bruises about their bodies, and as a deeper ache located somewhere under their ribs. But although it's still here, it's also gradually diminishing, being absorbed by the dynamics of the squad, by the recognition that the man next to you has been through what you've been through and is feeling what you're feeling.

The mark of a team is not just in how they win, but also in how they lose. How they use the memory of that loss as fuel and as knowledge. And how they use it to come closer, rather than fall apart. For Wales, at the end of this tour and a long run of rugby stretching back to those pre-World Cup sessions in Poland, this is how they are doing that today. Diffusing Thumper's funereal air of defeat by sharing in this wedding game, played out in a restaurant in Bondi as an Australian sun catches the waves on which the surfers ride, fall and swim back into, pushing themselves against the oncoming tide, to ride them again.

# ENGLAND

'The serpents began to struggle with each other; and the white one, raising himself up, threw down the other into the middle of the tent, and sometimes drove him to the edge of it; and this was repeated thrice. At length the red one, apparently the weaker of the two, recovering his strength, expelled the white one from the tent; and the latter being pursued through the pool by the red one, disappeared. Then the boy, asking the wise men what was signified by this wonderful omen, and they expressing their ignorance, he said to the king, "I will now unfold to you the meaning of this mystery. The pool is the emblem of this world, and the tent that of your kingdom: the two serpents are two dragons; the red serpent is your dragon, but the white serpent is the dragon of the people who occupy several provinces and districts of Britain, even almost from sea to sea: at length, however, our people shall rise and drive away the Saxon race from beyond the sea, whence they originally came."'

From *Historia Brittonum* by Nennius, ninth century (trans. J. A. Giles)

## Seasoned

April is the cruelest month, or so the poets said.
For us though it was autumn did the damage.
Thinning our wood with felled trees,
breaking our limbs in its storms.
As we entered winter's days
frost ran against our grain,
black with December rain.
But just as a coppiced trunk
confronts its cutting with growth,
and saplings will thicken into oaks,
so the torn muscle knits itself stronger
and the broken bone will heal itself firmer
to ready their bearers for the invitations of spring;
for the flexing of our boughs, the spreading of our wings.

When the Welsh players enter the home dressing room for their final match of the Six Nations, the tournament's trophy, stood on a table at the centre of J.R.'s folded towels and shirts, is waiting for them. Still Cybermanned in headphones, the players file past the silver cup to their changing stalls. Some are so focused on the match ahead they remain oblivious to its presence. Others, though, catch a glimpse of it out the corner of their eye and understand why it is there. For George North the sight is so unexpected it takes him a few seconds to realise what he's looking at. Once he does, he tries not to look at it again. On the coach journey from the Vale into Cardiff the squad have already been shown a video about the Grand Slam they won last year, and about how this trophy, wearing the red ribbons of Wales, is not so much theirs to win today as theirs to lose; a prize to be defended, not claimed.

To make this point manifest, Rob Howley has borrowed the trophy from the BBC and had it placed in the dressing room to be discovered, like a grail, when the team arrive. 'This trophy', he wants it to say to them as they change into their warm-up kit, 'is yours. This is where it belongs, in your stadium, so don't let anyone take it from you.' For those who've seen it as they entered, Rob's intention is effective; the final inspirational note in an orchestrated week of planning and preparation. As Richard Hibbard glances up at it from his stall, a 'Cymru' tattoo flexing across his shoulders as he pulls on his boots, he knows he'll do anything on the pitch today to make sure this trophy returns here after the game.

But for that to happen Wales must win, and the last five times they've walked into this home dressing room, they've lost. No other Welsh team has ever accumulated such a run of home defeats. Over their recent matches the sporting rule of 'home advantage' has become more of a curse than a blessing for Wales. But in sport, home is only ever half the story, and countering this run of losses is the fact that over the last two years Wales have won all of their away games in the Six Nations, beating every other team in the tournament on foreign turf.

It's a bizarre symmetry – five home defeats, five away victories – but such has been the nature of Wales's ugly duckling of a season so far. From a sombre defeat to Argentina last November, through yet another last-minute loss to Australia, to today's surprise title show-down against an ascendant England, Wales have, in the last five months, pushed themselves to the extremes of their wedding and funeral moments. In the process of doing so, they have changed. The team sheet today is largely the same as that which won the Grand Slam exactly a year ago. But the team itself is not, recast as they have been through a furnace of eight straight defeats before emerging back into their winning ways.

The autumn was especially dark. Despite leading 9–6 at half-time Wales could do nothing to hold back a dominant Argentina in the opening test of the autumn internationals. As the visiting Pumas outclassed them, Wales looked ponderous and tired. In contrast to the last time they'd played in Cardiff, beating France to win the Grand Slam, the double helix of crowd support and team performance became reversed. A subdued Wales created a subdued stadium which, in turn, further drained the players of energy. When they left the pitch, having lost 12–26, booing could be heard from the stands, a cruel reminder of the shortness of a crowd's memory, and of how in rugby, unless your present is perfect, your past counts for nothing at all.

Six days later, against Samoa, injury was added to insult, with Ian Evans, Richard Hibbard and Dan Biggar all leaving the field in the wake of the islanders' bouldering tackles. Even before the match began things were going wrong for Wales. When the players lined up to enter the tunnel, a cameraman opened a door to free a cable. As he did he created a backdraught, sucking in the dry ice through which the teams were meant to emerge. Within seconds the Welsh players were blinded by the billowing clouds filling the corridor, and had to enter the tunnel by feeling their way along the walls. It was an ominous start to the test, and one which proved all too prophetic when, just over a minute into the match, Samoa scored their first try in the corner. For the rest of the game the two sides traded a tight lead, but it was Samoa who took it into the eightieth minute, winning 26–19.

The following weekend New Zealand had almost achieved that same figure by half-time, Wales returning to their dressing room 23–0 behind. Once again Wales's injury list grew with their opponent's scoreline, Bradley Davies caught from behind by Andrew Hoare's swinging arm, Aaron Jarvis stretchered off and Jamie Roberts also helped from the field. But then, in the second half, something happened.

For forty minutes a different Wales seemed to take the field. New Zealand opened with another try, Luke Romano barging through Alex Cuthbert to touch down. But after that, the All Blacks would score no more. The slipped tackles and wary attacks melted from Wales's game, leaving a spikier version of the team that lined up at kick-off. When, in the fifty-seventh minute, Wales finally scored, they did so by combining their try with a telling moment of unity. Having once again used a penalty to kick for touch, Wales brought their entire team into the line-out. As Matthew Rees lifted his arms for the throw-in, the pitch to his right was an empty expanse of green, uninterrupted by the usual red-shirted diagonal. Wales were laying their cards on the table. They were taking this ball over the All Blacks' line, even if it meant using the whole team to do so. Which is exactly what they did, all fifteen players driving a maul to push Scott Williams over to score. Twenty minutes later, a more conventional move down the backline to the wing saw Alex Cuthbert go over in the corner.

The final score made far from pretty viewing, New Zealand winning 33–10, but Wales had shown a fighting spirit in their second-half performance. Under pressure and weakened by injury, they'd stemmed the bleeding of points to their opponents and finished the match scoring their own. Could they now, with the Wallabies coming to Cardiff, build on this performance and finally beat the team who'd so painfully denied them a victory three times on their Australian tour?

The answer, seven days later, was no. Once more what was starting to feel like the standard script for Wales vs Australia asserted itself. Australia, with Wales in the lead in the seventy-ninth minute, scored a try in the dying seconds to win the game 14–12. It was Wales's fourth successive defeat to the Wallabies in less than six months, with a total margin between the two teams of just thirteen points across the quartet of games. And it was, too, with the Six Nations just around the year's corner, Wales's fourth successive defeat at home. Grand Slam winners or not, as they left the field disheartened and beaten the months ahead of the Welsh players looked daunting and unkind, the upcoming defence of their title unlikely at best.

Wales's opponents today, England, had a very different close to their autumn series. Following defeats by Australia and South Africa, they pulled off a surprise 38–21 win over the All Blacks. Fuelled by this impressive victory, England have come to Cardiff today having won all of their previous matches in their Six Nations campaign. Because of this, as the English players enter their own dressing room down the corridor everything is on the table for them. Not just the trophy in the Welsh dressing room, but also the Triple Crown Wales won from them in Twickenham last year and, perhaps most tantalisingly, the first English Grand Slam in a decade. These are the prizes England have come to win, packing the hold of their coach not just with their kit and training equipment, but also with banners proclaiming 'England Grand Slam 2013' and cardboard boxes of T-shirts printed with the same. Their Six Nations has been far from perfect, but with the memory of that victory over the All Blacks still resonating, England are in confident mood. Many of the pundits, too, are backing them. Even before a single point had been scored, the commentators for their match against Italy last week were already talking of this game in Cardiff as being a Grand Slam decider.

What few foresaw, however, was that today's match would be a title decider too. The fact it is, is because

England failed to beat Italy by the kind of margin they'd hoped for, or which those commentators had predicted. When the final whistle blew in Twickenham, England, having failed to cross the tryline, had won by only seven points. Which means today Wales need to win by the same number to have a chance of retaining their title, and by just eight points to make sure of it.

That the match-day stars have aligned in this manner is, of course, due to Wales's previous victories in the tournament too. After losing to Ireland they went on to beat France, Italy and Scotland. But that first loss – and specifically the first half of that loss – has also played a crucial part in bringing Wales to the position they find themselves in this afternoon. It was a first half in which their opponents outplayed Wales to score twenty-three points to their three. But it was also, because of this, a forty minutes that gave Wales the trigger they needed to fire themselves back into form; a forty minutes which might have lost them a Grand Slam, but today might help them win a championship.

There is always pressure in international sport, but not all pressure is the same. A change of just a few degrees in the quality of the stresses upon a side can be transformative and often enough to be the difference between winning and losing. When Wales took the field against Ireland, they were Grand Slam defenders of the Six Nations. The prospect of winning a second clean sweep, back to back, was still in the air. Once again, after four successive home defeats, they were playing at home. The autumn internationals had been disappointing, but, their fans hoped, also an anomaly. Now the Six Nations had come round again they expected Wales to play as they had done in the tournament last year. Instead, and maybe exactly because of that expectation, they had to look on as Wales played what Mike Phillips later described as 'probably the worst forty minutes of Gatland's reign'.

Speaking about those forty minutes with hindsight, many of the players on the field that day talk about how they'd tried to play 'too much'. Rather than play the percentages and in the right areas of the field, rather than stick to a simple pattern when they had the ball, Wales tried to make every touch count. In doing so, as Jon Davies puts it, 'we put pressure on ourselves, instead of the opposition'.

While Ireland, deploying their choke tackles, successfully slowed down Wales's game, Wales failed to do the same. Their captain, Sam Warburton, usually so rapacious in the breakdown, didn't make a single turnover, the Irish double-teaming on him to clean him out every time. The same defensive errors that fractured the Welsh game plan in the autumn were still cracking their performance, leaving fissures for Ireland to exploit. When Simon Zebo deftly back-heeled a low pass to keep the ball in play, leading to a try by Cian Healy, the replayed image of his footwork before a beaten Welsh defence seemed emblematic of both the game so far and the game to come.

But then, as against New Zealand, the second half saw an unexpected turn in the story. As Wales emerged from an expletive-loud dressing room, they were determined, as George North put it, 'to just go at them'. That the team felt able to do this was primarily because of a change in the atmospheric pressure of the match. After a try by Brian O'Driscoll saw them trailing by twenty seven points, and with the hope of a second Grand Slam growing fainter by the second, the pressure upon Wales shifted, from one of expectation to one of aspiration. Combined with this was the fact that Wales were not intimidated by Ireland. They knew they were losing through their own failings, not their opponents' greater skill or power. They knew they were better than this.

When Wales, having answered O'Driscoll's try with three tries of their own, finally lost 22–30, it was that altered pressure that remained with them through the rest of the tournament; the kind of pressure, perhaps, under which Wales have always performed best. Not as Grand Slam defenders, but as competition contenders, facing an uphill struggle of three successive away matches and with their self-belief having to be proved all over again. As Richard Hibbard put it, speaking of those weeks following the defeat to Ireland, 'Pride's a horrible beast, and a lot changes when your pride's on the line.'

In Paris, with Ryan Jones taking the helm and Sam having to watch from home, with less than eight minutes left on the clock the two teams were still level at 6–6. But then a Dan Biggar chip, a George North charge, his left boot kept crucially suspended above the touchline as he scored, followed by Leigh Halfpenny's conversion from the same extreme angle, saw Wales win 16–6.

In the rain of Rome, by half-time Italy had already scored the same number of points France had taken a whole match to achieve, with Wales only three points ahead of them. Within another forty minutes, however, a further seventeen points were added to Wales's tally to bring them their second victory of the tournament, beating Italy 26–9.

In Scotland the rain might have stayed away, but the wind took its place, swirling in eddies and gusts around the stands of Murrayfield. Despite this, thirteen penalties were successfully kicked in the course of a match that saw a record eighteen attempted, with Leigh's boot and a blonde barge of a try by Hibbard bringing Wales a 28–18 victory. All of which, fuelled by that loss of points and pride against Ireland, has brought the Welsh players back to their home dressing room today, preparing to face England and just an eight-point margin away from keeping the trophy in the centre of the room theirs.

Not that they'll be chasing those eight points in the match ahead. To do so, Rob Howley has told them, would be a mistake. A win, that is all Wales want today. On their home ground, in front of their home fans, and over their old enemy. A win, their first in Cardiff since they beat France here a year ago. For a Welsh player, those are high enough stakes.

For the English players down the corridor, however, there is even more at stake, a win promising them a trinity of accolades that have eluded them for years, and which as a squad they've never yet tasted. Which is why, with less than an hour before kick-off, the pressures in the dressing rooms either side of the players' tunnel, despite the shared match ahead, are subtly different. And why of all the comparisons that have been flying around this week in the papers and online – of pack weights, metres carried, numbers of tackles – there is, perhaps, only one that really counts today: not how the teams compare head to head, but rather how they compare *in* their heads.

In terms of maturity, rugby years are something like dog years, accelerated versions of time. By age, the Welsh team, as they run out onto the pitch for their warm-up, are still relatively young. In rugby time, however, just two years after most of them first trained together, they are already a seasoned squad. They have seen and been through a lot. They've played across the globe, experienced landmark World Cup and Grand Slam matches. Today's starting fifteen have already, between them, taken the field for Wales 644 times.

In comparison, the English players who will line up opposite them, for all their power and talent, have a total of just 290 caps. A difference of 354 games and all the experience those playing minutes bring. Combined with this lack of international caps, few of them have ever played in Cardiff before, let alone in a title decider under a closed roof with a Welsh crowd singing to fill their opponents' sails.

This last factor, next to the hours of analysis, training, drills and nutrition that make up the modern rugby player, might seem insignificant. But rugby is an emotional game, in which the inches of the heart and mind are every bit as important as the inches of a bicep or a thigh. Which is why the Welsh players appreciate just what an advantage the emotional narrative of the day might be for them. That even if their fans can't join them on the field to play their part in a victory, they'll more than sing their part in one from the stands.

When, in the week running up to the match, Rob Howley learnt England were coming to Cardiff to play a running game, one of his selection dilemmas was immediately solved for him. All through the tournament there'd been a debate in Wales over who should wear the number-seven shirt. Following the Australian tour and the defeat to Ireland, Sam's form and confidence had dipped, only to rally last week against Scotland. Justin Tipuric's, however, had remained strong throughout the campaign. All week the question of who would play at seven against England had been one of the most recurrent in the media. But now Rob knew. Both Sam and Justin would be in the starting line-up. For the first time, to counter England's intentions, both sevens would play from the kick-off, with Sam switching to six. Which is why, as the subs line up in the corridor and the team gather in a huddle in the dressing room, as they bind tight and listen to the muffled stands above them, both Sam and Justin are in the circle, stamping their feet, listening to their captain's final words of encouragement.

That captain isn't Ryan Jones, who broke his shoulder against Scotland. And nor is it Sam himself, who, having won man of the match last week under Ryan, has chosen to play again unfettered by the responsibility. For this game of all games, rather than worry about coin tosses and penalty decisions, Sam just wants, in his words, 'to listen to my crazy music for an hour and then go out and smash the opposition'. So instead it is Wales's veteran prop, Gethin Jenkins, who is leaning into the circle of his teammates, who is looking each of them in the eye and reminding them what is expected of them today, and of how hard, but how worth it, it will be to achieve.

Gethin will be Wales's most experienced player on the field today, winning his ninety-eighth cap the moment his boot touches the stadium's turf. As such, over the last week he's been able to take the occasion of today's match in his stride. Along with the rest of the squad, isolated out in the Vale, he's managed to escape the debate and anticipation fevering the rest of the country. But even with this most grounded of squads, there is only so long the symbolic stature of today's match can be kept at bay.

As they prepare to enter the tunnel, Justin Tipuric, for whom nerves are never usually a problem, knows he is more nervous than ever before. Since early this morning he's been receiving texts and messages from friends and family asking him to do Wales proud, asking him to beat the English, each one of them ratcheting up a coil of tightly wound anticipation. Dan Biggar, meanwhile, has been aware, over these last minutes before they take the field, of a new kind of nervous voltage energising the Wales dressing room. He's played in other big matches, and he's experienced nervous dressing rooms before, in which the nerves translate and spread through a team in such a way as to shake their focus and resolve. But today is different to anything he's ever known before. 'It just kept building,' is how he described it months later. 'This nervous energy, building and building.'

For all their experience, when Wales finally emerge from the tunnel and enter the stadium, none of the team are prepared for what is waiting for them. The volume and passion of the crowd are greater than any they've heard before. To a man, as they bind about each other's shoulders for the anthems, none of them have ever heard them sung as the crowd sing them now. The meaning of the day has finally found its voice, and the players must use all their psychological strength to not let it throw them off balance. Because with all their 644 caps, with all their knowledge of rugby and Wales, this, these seconds and minutes, is still an experience beyond any they've known – to witness and be the focus of the sheer power and *calon* of this home crowd, its fires stoked today as much by the promise of what Wales might deny an unbeaten England as by what Wales might themselves win.

There are certain games that become protean with time, shifting under the influence of memory. Wales vs England on 16 March 2013 has already become one of those games. Played in the wake of an autumn and winter of discontent, and refracted through the final score of Wales's 30–3 victory, the game is now remembered, in Wales at least, as a rout – a display of superior Welsh power and rugby intelligence over a younger and inexperienced England.

But for most of the eighty minutes the match was much harder and closer than that. It was intense, fast-paced and physical. Wales played with both imagination and accuracy, but the dramatic imbalance of that final scoreline was far from a foregone conclusion. In the second half, with less than thirty minutes to go Wales were still only 9–3 in the lead and still adrift of the championship, with England only a couple of scores away from snatching a victory.

From kick-off the emotion, history and stakes of the game were translated into its pace. At fourteen minutes Richard Hibbard looked up at the clock, expecting it to be close to half-time. At twenty-five minutes, as Jonathan

Davies walked back into the line he looked at the Welsh forwards and thought, 'Christ, they look as if they need oxygen!' But this had always been part of Wales's game plan: to back their own fitness and, in the knowledge that England had had a day less recovery time than them, keep them moving, keep them tackling. Take quick free kicks and whenever possible keep the ball in play. Because if the Welsh players were struggling with the game's pace, then at least they could be sure the English players were too, and that eventually something would have to give.

The one area where Wales didn't have to wait for England to give was in their scrummaging. From the first time the two sides packed down five minutes into the game, Wales, with the Australian Steve Walsh officiating, had the upper hand. Again and again through the first half the guile of Adam Jones, backed by the power of the Welsh pack behind him, had the English front row splintering out of shape like tectonic plates creating mountain ranges. It was these set pieces, along with the Welsh forward play at the breakdown, that fed Wales's first nine points, with Leigh slotting a series of penalties to take them six points ahead. Psychologically, too, the Welsh forwards were laying down the foundation for their victory. When, after yet another defeat at the scrum, Dan Cole grabbed Hibbard around the neck, Hibbard didn't mind. It was, in a way, what they'd all been waiting for; a sign they were getting to England, that they were winning the mind as well as the muscle game.

Despite this domination at the scrum, and a series of penetrating attacks from Mike Phillips, Jonathan Davies and George North, those three penalties remained Wales's only points of the first half. England defended and attacked with furious intent. Their own fans had travelled west with them, and despite being outnumbered 'Swing Low' frequently countered 'Hymns and Arias' throughout the half. At forty minutes, with the clock turned red, Dan Biggar attempted a drop goal to silence both English singers and players. But the ball fell agonisingly short, and Wales had to return to their dressing room in the lead, but still not by enough to win the championship.

That margin was finally breached at fifty-one minutes fifty-one seconds as, following a rapid chain of Welsh phases, England were once again penalised at the breakdown. In return Leigh took a further three points off them with his boot. Somehow, after the darkness of those days in autumn, Wales were there. Few outside the core of the squad had dared believe it could happen, but if the score now remained the same, Wales, from the ashes of that Irish defeat, would win the Six Nations for a second year in a row.

As it turned out, the score did not remain the same. England, in response to the prospect of not only losing their Grand Slam, but also the competition, switched two-thirds of their front row for fresh blood, then launched a blistering attack. Just as Wales had relentlessly driven forward to win that penalty, so now they had to be equally resolute in their defence. For several minutes red shirts felled white as English player after English player smashed into them, recycled the ball, and came at them again. Eventually, as Wales had always hoped, their attacking pattern broke. Once more it was the Welsh forwards who created the foundations. From out of the rhythm of charges Adam Jones took the legs of Tom Wood, the English number eight. Ken Owens, meanwhile, jackalled at his arms to free the ball, sending it spinning into the hands of the waiting Justin Tipuric, who in turn passed it from the breakdown's tight knot to Mike Phillips and the open spaces of the Welsh backline.

In eight more seconds, it was done, the ball reaching Alex Cuthbert at the line's end, who handed off and outpaced England's Mike Brown to score in the corner. Leigh missed the conversion, but as the game started again Wales were 17–3 in the lead, and whatever it is that vitalises a team's spirit began to bleed away from the English players. A momentum graph of the match clearly illustrates this draining of their energy. Up until Alex's try the lines of both teams are equal. But after it, while Wales's momentum remains steady, England's begins to fall, curving away towards the final whistle.

From here on in, Wales's performance was a lesson in chipping away at an opponent's morale. Within a few minutes Dan Biggar succeeded where he'd failed before, and scored a drop goal. Once again England responded to a Welsh score with a rash of fresh substitutes, only for one of them, Danny Care, to miss Sam when he broke from a ruck to charge downfield. Like a pack of wolves the crowd scented blood in Sam's freeing sprint, and as their voices rose the ball flicked through Welsh hands again – Phillips, Biggar, Halfpenny, Roberts, Tipuric, who, showing the muscle memory of his teenage years playing in the backs, dummied Mike Brown before offloading to Cuthbert to score almost exactly where he had just ten minutes earlier.

The rest has become Welsh rugby history. Biggar's conversion, then his scoring of yet another penalty, followed by a Welsh defence which continued to absorb a barrage of English bodies, delivered a final score of Wales 30, England 3. In doing so, another strange symmetry was bestowed upon Wales's Six Nations tournament. That same score, weighted against them versus Ireland, had been the turning point in both their pressure and their resolve. Driven on from that low by that low, Rob Howley's Wales had somehow managed to put the memory of eight straight defeats behind them, and make one of the most dramatic comebacks the game has ever known.

The following day the newspapers were full of praise for both coach and team. Alongside many of the match reports, however, were reminders of just how unexpected this win had been. Advertisers, having to plan in advance, and in the hope of catching the reflected glory of a Grand Slam, had put their money behind England. 'They mean business. We mean business,' an insurer's advert proclaimed in the *Telegraph*. Next to this copy was a photograph of the same English front row Wales had taken apart the day before. Above the advert's predictive hope the paper's headline – 'Wales Shatter England' – told a different story. A story of however much business England might have meant, on the day it was Wales who'd meant better business and England who'd had to return defeated, their boxes of celebratory T-shirts still unpacked in the hold of their coach.

# LIONS

The British and Irish Lions are that sporting anomaly, a geographical rather than national team. Its players share no capital city, no anthem, no flag. They are a team with no home ground, who've only ever played their test matches on foreign soil. They are an invasion of a side, in which the blend of players from four nations is both their greatest strength and their greatest weakness. A team which only appears, like a returning comet, once every four years.

The inherited bond of the players who fill out the Lions shirts is one of climate more than culture. A rugby heritage of being the best, combined with a shared history of being islanders; a group of men defined by shorelines, not borders. As such, despite the commercial paraphernalia of merchandising, branding and TV adverts there is still something elemental in the idea of the Lions. Something enduring.

For the last sixteen years, however, there has also been something disappointing. Over four successive tours the Lions, drawing on the most talented players these islands have to offer, have failed to defeat any of their southern-hemisphere hosts. In 2013, facing a tour to Australia, it was with breaking this historical pattern Warren Gatland was tasked when he was chosen as the touring party's coach. And it was with this goal in mind, and no other, that he selected his squad.

Perhaps unsurprisingly, given Gatland was watching in Cardiff at that Six Nations decider in March, when his selection was made, fifteen Welsh players, an entire starting line-up, comprised the largest single contribution to the squad. For these Welsh players the Lions tour, as well as being a pinnacle in the story of their careers, also provided them an opportunity to bring their rugby year to a close by subverting their own recent history against the Wallabies; the chance to expunge those painfully close losses of their whitewash tour twelve months earlier with a series win, this time in the red shirt of the Lions, if not Wales.

Gatland's Lions knew how they wanted to bring such a series victory about: by making sure of it in the first and second tests and not waiting for the third. Too often Lions tours had come down to that last match, leaving everything on the line for those final minutes of rugby. The Lions wanted to put the Australians to bed quickly, and definitively, then enjoy the denouement of their tour, secure in the knowledge of their success.

But once in Australia, the 2013 tourists found the tide of history still strong, and instead they were handed exactly the series structure they'd hoped to avoid. In the first test a last-minute missed kick by Kurtley Beale lost the Wallabies the match, 21–23. But in the second, it was Leigh's turn to have his own last-minute penalty fall short, and the turn of the Lions to lose, 15–16. All meaning that as the squad approached the third and final test in Sydney, the series stood undecided at 1–1, and sixteen years of defeats still cast a shadow over the Lions coaches and players alike.

On the morning of 3 July Warren Gatland gathered his squad to announce the team for the third test. When that same team sheet was announced to the press, it caused consternation and even outrage throughout the rugby-watching world. Keith Wood, the ex-Ireland and Lions hooker, declared Gatland had made 'a terrible mistake'. Willie John McBride, the most-capped Lion ever, was worried the Lions ethos was slipping and thought the Australian coach Robbie Deans 'must be laughing all the way'.

Gatland had selected ten Welsh players in the starting line-up. Two-thirds of the team would come from west of Offa's Dyke. Bancyfelin, a tiny village in Carmarthenshire, could claim, in Jonathan Davies and Mike Phillips, to have contributed more players to the third test side than all of Scotland put together. But although this Welsh bias attracted some criticism and comment, it was the decision around a single player, not ten, that provoked such a strong reaction as to suggest Gatland hadn't so much made a tactical error as an emotional mistake.

For the first time in Brian O'Driscoll's fifteen-year international career, a coach had dropped the veteran Irish centre. Not just from the starting line-up, but from the entire third-test squad. With Jamie Roberts recovered from injury, Gatland had moved the in-form Jon Davies to his preferred position of outside centre and brought Jamie in at number twelve. The bulk of Manu Tuilagi took the centre's place on the bench.

At thirty-four years old, and a member of three previous losing Lions tours, playing in a winning third test would have been both the crowning moment and the ultimate curtain call of O'Driscoll's career. And this, it seems, is what triggered the acres of newsprint, online comments and debate. There was a rugby argument for O'Driscoll's inclusion in the side – his experience, his communication skills, the combination of his subtlety on the shoulder of Jamie's battering ram that worked so well on the Lions tour in 2009. But it was a question of narrative more than rugby that stirred up such a chorus of passionate voices against Gatland's decision. There are stories of teams, his critics seemed to be saying, and there are stories of matches. But then there are also stories of players. In not selecting O'Driscoll, Gatland had denied the Irish centre his perfect ending. He had, it was felt, stolen his story.

In the fervour of their support for O'Driscoll, Gatland's detractors seemed to have been blinded to the opposing rugby argument for the selection choices he'd made.

As Gatland said himself at the press conference when he announced the team, he'd had to go with 'head over heart'. Had the series stood, as he'd hoped it would, at 2–0, then there's every chance O'Driscoll would have got his game. But it didn't, so Gatland had to pick the team he thought would win. And that meant trusting to both form and established playing combinations.

The blending of national styles, of pairings that would be impossible in any other team, is part of the Lions ethos. Their very existence is a celebration of the difference and unity of playing four nations as one. But such untried pairings can also be a risk. In the second test Ben Youngs at scrum-half and Jonny Sexton at outside-half had only ever played thirty minutes of test rugby together before facing Australia. The combination didn't fire, and the team suffered as a result. Jamie and Jon, however, had played hundreds, if not thousands, of hours together, on the training pitch as well as on the international stage. Added to this was the fact that Jon had been one of the stand-out successes of the tour so far, playing more minutes than any other member of the party. His passing game had improved and, despite playing out of position, combined with his physicality and fitness he'd more than put his hand up as a contender for the number-thirteen shirt. O'Driscoll himself had spotted this as early as the match against New South Wales. When the final whistle went, he'd commented to Adam Jones on how well Jon had played.

'He's good, isn't he?' he'd said. 'I'd better watch out.'

Gatland made sure to let O'Driscoll know of his decision before the team announcement. Once it was made, the Irishman congratulated Jamie and Jon, and offered to help bring Jamie up to speed on calls and plays. Within the wider squad, too, as a senior player he continued to play a crucial role, making speeches of encouragement, offering advice and reminding the players chosen to represent the Lions that after experiencing three defeats, even if he wasn't playing himself, he desperately wanted this series win. 'This is my fourth crack at it,' he told the assembled squad. 'And my last one, and I want it so fucking badly.'

The other surprise of Gatland's team announcement was his choice of captain. For the first two tests, having chosen to relinquish the captaincy of Wales during the Six Nations, Sam had rediscovered his confidence to lead the Lions. Just a few months earlier, following some weak performances and negative press, he'd been finding it increasingly difficult to convince himself of his pre-match identity statement – 'I am the best number seven in the world.' But after his man-of-the-match performance against Scotland, and then the win over England, Sam was back to his playing best when Gatland asked him to captain the Lions. He didn't hesitate in saying yes. To be asked, he said, was 'pure joy'. When Sam was sixteen, his parents had bought him a replica Lions shirt. He'd worn it all the time, until one day he'd decided he wouldn't wear it again. When his father had asked him why, Sam told him it was because he wanted the next Lions shirt he wore to be the real thing. And it was, with Sam starting as captain in the first two tests of the tour.

For this final test, however, a torn hamstring meant he couldn't take the helm. With O'Driscoll out of the side, the role of captain was left wide open. Again, Gatland went with what he knew and chose Alun Wyn Jones as his skipper. It was an astute choice. Those in the squad who'd played under Alun Wyn for the Ospreys knew he was a captain who would lead from the front, who'd put his body on the line for a win and who'd infect the team with his passion.

A Lions squad is about a blending not only of playing character, but also of national character, and in this respect, too, in a starting line-up of predominately Welsh and Irish players, Alun Wyn was a canny choice. The Welsh dressing room before a game is a surprisingly quiet place. Players like Toby Faletau, Leigh Halfpenny, Jon Davies are not big talkers before a match, preferring to centre themselves quietly. In contrast, the Irish players in the squad are used to a talkative dressing room; to leaders like Paul O'Connell, Brian O'Driscoll and Jamie Heaslip fuelling the team's engine with a constant flow of words. Of the Welsh players, Alun Wyn is by far the most vocal, and as such promised to bridge this stylistic divide across the Irish Sea well. As a forward, and with the game likely to be fought and penalised up front and at the breakdown, he'd also be a captain at the coalface of both the playing and the refereeing. A 'Big Red Machine', as he calls himself, at the front line of the game.

Not that everyone saw things quite the same way. Along with the criticism aimed at him for dropping O'Driscoll, Gatland also had to absorb a fair amount of flak for his choice of captain. The only advantage to this was that in the run-up to the test, as well as being the squad's coach, Gatland also became its diversion. With the rugby press going after him, the players themselves could stay out of the line of fire, and go after the game instead. For Jon Davies, though, this was an especially difficult week. He'd fought long and hard to overcome injury, and then failures in his own performance, to bring himself to this position – starting a deciding test for the Lions. And now he was, the focus wasn't on his deserving his position, but rather on how he'd unjustly taken O'Driscoll's place. He had, in the last few days, become rugby's public enemy number one. When his family came to take him out for a coffee on the eve of the game, they tried to make light of it, his parents asking Jon to walk a few paces behind them when they left the hotel. But beneath this joke they knew the reaction to the team announcement meant that the match ahead, as well as deciding the series, now bore another, more personal pressure for their son. One that was comprised not just of the prospect of his taking part in a future victory, but also of justifying himself in the light of O'Driscoll's past.

In a more general sense this variety of pressure is one which every international player carries with him onto the field. The accumulated weight of all those other players not selected for your position. The other men who'd give anything to be wearing your shirt, who could easily, given another throw of the dice, have had your number on their back. The only answer to this weight, though, is your own performance, your own success. And in a way, this is also what each of the selected Lions was hoping to win at that third test in Sydney. Not just the match, the series and a place in rugby history, but also their proven right to have been the chosen man. As Jamie Roberts told the squad's 'player cam' on the morning of the test, 'It's about doing what you can for your mate next to you and just giving it your all. Because if you don't, you're doing thousands of rugby players back home a huge injustice.'

## Lions vs Australia, Third Test
## 6 July 2013

There are just a few minutes to kick-off and only the team are left in the dressing room. The coaches have gone to their glass-walled box, the subs are lining the corridor. Just the starting fifteen remain, huddled in a circle.

It is evening in Sydney and all day the players binding about each other's shoulders have been waiting for this. Alun Wyn, their captain, unhooks his arm from George North's neck and leans in to speak to his team. His face is reddened from the warm-up but he speaks steadily, calmly, his finger pointing his words in the air. 'No separation in defence, no separation in attack. Keep moving. Don't be lazy.'

His voice rises, in volume, in determination.

'To put it into one thing: don't give up. And that's not on the sixty or sixty-five, it's from the fucking first minute to the fucking eighty plus.'

His voice rises again, more urgent, more demanding.

'You don't give up. On a kick-chase. On a jackal. On filling in. You don't give up on anything! For eighty minutes!'

Now he is shouting, beating his free hand as a fist.

'The biggest mark of respect you can have is to be fucking pulled off, blowing out your arse, with nothing left to give.'

He looks around at the men looking back at him. When he speaks to them again, there is a vein pulsing at his temple. 'Do not give up on anything!'

The first touch is a mistake, and perfect.

Will Genia, the Australian scrum-half who'd so harried Wales on their tour, and now the Lions on theirs, knocks the ball on from Sexton's kick-off.

The forwards pack down for the first scrum, but the Wallabies are penalised for early engagement. The whistle is still in the referee's lips when Mike Phillips, who has fought all tour against a knee injury to be here tonight, taps the free kick and runs. Immediately, he worries he's gone too soon. But now it is also too late.

The Lions link a chain of pick and drives together. With each one they gain metres, until, with just over a minute played, their captain, Alun Wyn, is already being brought down inches short of the Australian line. Mike passes again, this time to Alex Corbisiero, who is tackled, rolls, and plants the ball to score. One minute sixteen seconds, and the Lions have first blood.

Leigh converts. 7–0.

Australia, wanting revenge, refuse an opportunity to kick

for goal and go for the corner instead. From the line-out they launch darting attacks. As the Wallaby flanker George Smith tries to break through he is tackled by Alun Wyn. At the same moment, he clashes heads with Hibbard. The impact is so hard the sound of their collision is picked up by the referee's mike, a sickening crack. Hibbard, thinking he's been bounced, jumps back to his feet. But Smith remains prone. A minute later he is led from the field.

Ten minutes and four penalties later and the score stands at 16–3 to the Lions. A pattern has been established. A scrum is called, the Lions pack dominate, Australia are penalised. When the statistics are gathered at the end of this match, many of them will illustrate the parity of the teams, the tightness of the margins.

### Defenders beaten
Lions – 19                   Australia – 18
### Missed tackles
Lions – 18                   Australia – 19
### Turnovers won
Lions – 8                    Australia – 7

But one will tell a different story:

### Scrums won/lost
Lions – 10/0                 Australia – 3/3

This is the foundation of the Lions' game. The outward result of the hidden work of the front row, chipping away at their opposite numbers to undermine Australia's momentum.

Australia attack again. The Lions turn the ball over. Leigh clears upfield, and there, true to his word, the first red shirt chasing the ball into the Wallabies twenty-two is the Lions' captain, Alun Wyn.

A verse of 'Bread of Heaven' washes through the stands.

Australia choose, again, to kick for the corner, not goal. From the line-out the fuse of their backline burns all the way to Israel Folau on the wing.

Of all the rugby players with whom Frans Bosch, the biomechanics expert, has worked, the two most natural athletes he has ever met are Israel Folau, who now accelerates towards the Lions' line, and George North, who is waiting for him.

Across all the tests this has been one of the most contested head-to-head battles. In the second test George stunned viewers across the world, and many of his teammates on the pitch, when he replied to Folau's attempt to tackle him by hitching him in a fireman's lift and continuing his run, carrying both man and ball.

Now, as Folau picks up speed, the two giant wingers meet again, with George once more not just tackling Folau, but picking him off the ground and driving him towards the touchline. Folau offloads, his passage, this time, cut short.

The pace does not slacken. Australia continue to opt for scrums or line-outs over kicks at goal. Leigh sweeps up their long clearances. Alun Wyn, Dan Lydiate and Hibbard tackle relentlessly, and Sean O'Brien recycles the ball with speed for Mike to start it all over again.

The next score, however, follows the established pattern of the match. A scrum, Australia's Ben Alexander yellow-carded, Leigh's boot harvesting another three points.

The Lions 19, Australia 3. The third test – and, it seems, the series – will be theirs.

But the Wallabies, as the Welsh players know all too well, are last-minute masters. And sure enough, with the scoreline remaining unchanged for the rest of the half, it is only when the clock is red that their fightback begins.

The Lions have already extinguished several dangerous breaks, most notably when Geoff Parling had to stretch himself to his full length to bring down a sprinting Jesse Mogg, his tap tackle catching the Australian's ankle just in time.

But Mogg's break is a sign of the Wallabies' intent. They want to close the divide before half-time. They want to chase the game, choosing five times not to kick for goal and turning their backs on fifteen possible points in the process.

It's from the final scrum of the half that O'Connor, the Australian fly-half, cuts and jinks past four Lions defenders to score to the right of the posts, the clock at 41:20. Australia convert, and the Lions return to their dressing room nine points in the lead but still just a converted try and a kick from losing the test, the series and their pride.

In the dressing room, voices are kept low. Unlike the shouted statements and directions before the game, advice is given more quietly now, softly even, as the players listen, take on fluid and try to regain control of their breathing. Forwards coach Graham Rowntree crouches among his players. 'Let's make a pact now,' he asks them. 'We don't let them up. We've got a foot on them and we keep them fucking down on the canvas.' Defence coach Andy Farrell, like a school teacher in the middle of an attentive class, tells the whole team, 'Let them play four or five phases, right? And keep knocking them back, right? I'll tell you why, because this game is only about momentum, right?'

When the coaches have returned to their box high in the stands, Alun Wyn gathers his fifteen into a circle once more and asks them to imagine themselves to a win. 'We are the team that's behind.' He taps his temple. 'Keep that in your mind. We're at home, and we're behind, yeah?'

But everything said in the dressing room is just words. However much the players listen, however much they repeat those words, they are still only words and meaningless unless translated into action. Australia, though, will not let this happen. Having closed the scoreline with a try in the first half, they now stitch it closer and closer with first one penalty, then another.

Six minutes into the second half, and the Wallabies, for all the words in the Lions dressing room, are breathing down their necks, the scoreline standing at 19–16.

Leigh replies with a penalty of his own. But it is five minutes later, after a rash of injuries to the Lions' forwards, as Leigh beats two Australian defenders and offloads inside to Sexton, that the game finally breaks in the Lions' favour. Leigh's offload is made just five metres from the Australian line, leaving Sexton to cross it unmolested and score under the posts.

It is Leigh who is at the birth of the Lions' next try too, gathering an Australian kick to beat two defenders before offloading, this time on his outside to George, who outpaces O'Connor to score in the corner.

In the stands, dressed in his number ones, Brian O'Driscoll is smiling. Around him the night air of Sydney is lifted with 'Bread of Heaven' again, stronger this time, sung in celebration, not hope.

The Lions' fourth try is also scored by a Welshman, Jamie Roberts, who was told his chances of staying on the tour, following an injury, were only fifty–fifty. With Owen Farrell running at a dummy angle, and George distracting another three of the opposition, Jamie sprints in from deep to link with Conor Murray and slice through the Australian defence. Handing off Will Genia, he crosses the line to score.

Leigh converts the try, to bring his personal tally on the tour to 114, an astonishing 30 per cent of all the points the Lions will score in Australia.

The Lions now lead Australia by 41–16, and for once versus the Wallabies, that is how the scoreline remains until the final whistle. When that whistle is blown, for the first time in sixteen years the Lions, many of them with blood blushing their white collars, have won a test series. In celebration the players find each other on the field, the rest of the touring party joining them, and hug each other; the same men who just months before were Six Nations rivals now embracing in a shared victory on foreign soil.

For the Welsh players among them the scene is full of echoes. The sea of red in the stands is a colour of support they know all too well. The chant of 'Lions, Lions', meanwhile, sounds the same percussive rhythm as the 'Wales, Wales' that heartbeats the Millennium Stadium back home. The rhythm of the match they've just played, too, is familiar, its contours and turning points mapping almost exactly their Six Nations win against England. Even the grim faces and dejected body language of the

Australian players are an echo of a kind, a reminder of their own dejection in this stadium a year ago; of how far and how quickly rugby fortunes can rise and fall and rise again.

For all of them, this charged moment of their victory, already slipping second by second into their pasts, is also the climax of their personal journeys in the sport. Journeys that root back to multiple pitches and gyms and villages in Wales. To silent hours alone, icing their limbs. To rusted stands in high southern valleys singing with wind. To the men and women, the coaches, parents and teachers, who said the words of encouragement that made them believe. To that spark of desire when they first saw a game played, and wanted to play.

As the Lions squad complete their lap of honour and filter back into their dressing room, Adam Jones, a tighthead prop from Abercrave, remains on the field. Slowly, he walks its borders, looking up at the terraced stands for his wife and daughter. He does not find them. The stadium is still packed, and everyone wants a piece of him, a photograph, an autograph, a souvenir of the memory. So eventually Adam, too, turns and makes his way back to the dressing room and his celebrating teammates. But even though he hasn't found his wife and daughter among the thousands, Adam still knows they are up there somewhere, watching from the crowded stands. And he knows, too, that this is what is important. That Isla has seen him play today, in this match of all matches, and that in the years to come, it will be this that matters. As it will for all of them – the fans, the players, the coaches. That when those eighty minutes of pure present, with the blowing of a whistle, instantly became a piece of historic rugby past, they were there. They made the journey, turned up, and were there.

# ACKNOWLEDGEMENTS

This book would not have been possible without the Arts Council Wales/WRU Artist in Residence scheme, and I am particularly grateful to Dai Smith and Roger Lewis for having the vision to create such a project with the aim of bringing the cultures of sport and the arts closer together in Wales. Over the last year I have been fortunate enough to spend time with both the national squad and several other teams across Wales. I would like to thank all the players and coaches who have granted me interviews and allowed me such a privileged insight into Welsh rugby and their lives. I am especially grateful to the players and coaches of the Wales tour to Australia for allowing me into their camp with such openness, and to Thumper for assimilating me into the logistical details of the tour.

As well as my first-hand research, several books and DVDs have been invaluable in providing a broader context for *Calon*, including: *Fields of Praise: The Official History of the Welsh Rugby Union 1881–1981* by Dai Smith and Gareth Williams (Cardiff University Press, 1980); *A Game for Hooligans: The History of Rugby Union* by Huw

Richards (Mainstream, 2006); *The Welsh Grand Slam 2012* by Paul Rees (Mainstream, 2012); *Library of Wales, Sport* edited by Gareth Williams (Parthian, 2007); *Rugby's Strangest Matches* by John Griffiths (Robson Books for Past Times); *Life at Number 10* by Neil Jenkins with Paul Rees (Mainstream, 1998); *Number Nine Dream* by Rob Howley with Graham Clutton (Mainstream, 1999); *Lions Triumphant; The Captain's Story* by Sam Warburton with Steve James (Simon & Schuster, 2013); *Lions Raw* (Stamp Productions).

I am also grateful to the following estates, authors and publishers for permission to quote from the following material: Sheenagh Pugh from her poem 'Toast', (*The Beautiful Lie*, Seren, 2002); Faber & Faber from Ted Hughes's letter (*The Letters of Ted Hughes* edited by Christopher Reid, Faber & Faber, 2007), from Seamus Heaney's 'Postscript' (*The Spirit Level*, Faber & Faber, 1996) and from T. S. Eliot's *The Four Quartets*; the estate of R. S. Thomas for quotations from 'A Peasant' and 'Song at the Year's Turning' (© Kunjana Thomas, 2001); The Blims for quotations from 'Sidesteps and Sideburns' (www.theblims.co.uk); V2 Music for quotations from Stereophonics' 'Is Yesterday, Tomorrow, Today?'; Eric Clapton for quotations from his song 'Wonderful Tonight' © 1970 Eric Clapton; and Universal Music for quotations from Anthrax's 'Refuse to Be Denied'.

I would like to thank, as ever, my agent, Zoe Waldie, and my editor at Faber, Lee Brackstone, both of whom have supported me now for over a decade. I'm also grateful to Anne Owen for overseeing a tight production schedule with such understanding, and to Ian Bahrami for his quick and thorough eye. Lastly, thanks to Ryan for letting me off when I lost at table tennis, and to Katherine Eluned, for the listening, the reading, the advice and for being there.

*Also by Owen Sheers*

ff

## Resistance

It's 1944 and the D-Day landings have failed. Sarah Lewis wakes up to find herself alone – her husband has disappeared, along with all the men in her Welsh border valley. As the women work to run the farms throughout the winter, a German patrol arrives, led by Captain Albrecht Wolfram. Cut off from the surrounding war, the lines between collaboration, occupation and survival become blurred for Sarah and Albrecht, and everyone in the valley must decide what is worth fighting for.

'At once a brilliant and sometimes frightening thriller, and a mature exploration of human blur and compromise.' GUARDIAN

'A moving meditation on what war does to people . . . Impossible to resist.' FINANCIAL TIMES

'A moving story of loyalty and quiet courage.' OBSERVER

# ff

# The Dust Diaries

When Owen Sheers discovers a book in his father's study, he stumbles upon the life of an obscure relative: Arthur Cripps, lyric poet and maverick missionary to Rhodesia. Compelled by the description of Cripps's extraordinary life in Africa, Sheers embarks on a journey through contemporary Zimbabwe in an attempt to better understand his ancestor's devotion to the country and its people, and the dramatic, often bloody, differences that echo across the years.

'A truly wonderful book.' Doris Lessing, TLS BOOKS OF THE YEAR

'This is a slow-burning, mesmerising book that snags the heart with a telling detail or murmured regret then opens its gaze to reveal a wider, bolder view of time and place and history, like a camera lens taking in a shimmering veld.' INDEPENDENT ON SUNDAY

'Sheers is a vivid, sensuous writer . . . the impetuousness, curiosity and zest of the narrative are compelling, and suggest the force that drove Cripps also drives this young man.' THE TIMES

'In style *The Dust Diaries* is beautifully elegiac, at times reaching a mystical intensity, but it is never sentimental or pretentious. Sheers writes with warm admiration for his extraordinary ancestor.' LITERARY REVIEW ff

## Pink Mist

A work of great dramatic power, documentary integrity and emotional intensity, *Pink Mist* uses everyday yet heightened speech to excavate the human cost of modern warfare. Drawing upon interviews with soldiers and their families, as well as ancient texts such as the medieval Welsh poem *Y Gododdin*, it is the first extended lyric narrative to emerge from the devastating conflict in Afghanistan.

Shortlisted for the BBC Audio Drama Awards 2013, *Pink Mist* displays all of Owen Sheers's virtuoso gifts for language and poetic drama.

'Owen Sheers' breath-taking, unforgettable script focuses on the abused lives of three British soldiers with the humanity of a Wilfred Owen poem and brings the pity of the far Afghan war into our own mind's neighbourhood.' Dannie Abse

'*Pink Mist* is a tremendous book. It feels huge, engulfing, devastating, although only 87 pages long. When I finished it, what I felt most strongly was that it should be studied at school alongside the ubiquitous Wilfred Owen.' Kate Kellaway, OBSERVER

'The war poet of our generation.' INDEPENDENT

'Hugely atmospheric and affecting . . . Masterfully controlling rhyme and rhythm, Sheers tunnels through the darkness to display the triumph of love and language over violence and silence.' Anitha Sethi, INDEPENDENT

'The verse becomes threnody, a lyrical lament. Sheers does not judge; this is a work going far beyond simple ideological stances. The best analogue to *Pink Mist* is *In Parenthesis* by David Jones, magician, creator and rifleman . . . Owen Sheers can stand the comparison.' Peter Scupham, LITERARY REVIEW

'Owen Sheers' phenomenal new book *Pink Mist* is riveting, relevant British writing . . . contemporary in its points of reference and timeless in its depiction of the pity of war. It is both utterly convincing and extremely moving, devastating even.' Alex Blimes, ESQUIRE

'The first important poem to come out of Britain's most recent Afghan war, there's more truth, more power to disturb, in Owen Sheers' *Morte d'Arthur* than in acres of media coverage.' PN REVIEW